Mexican Raiders
in the Major Leagues

ALSO BY G. RICHARD MCKELVEY
AND FROM MCFARLAND

*All Bat, No Glove:
A History of the Designated Hitter* (2004)

*For It's One, Two, Three, Four Strikes You're Out
at the Owners' Ball Game: Players Versus
Management in Baseball* (2001)

*The Bounce: Baseball Teams'
Great Falls and Comebacks* (2001)

*The MacPhails: Baseball's First Family
of the Front Office* (2000)

*Fisk's Homer, Willie's Catch
and the Shot Heard Round the World:
Classic Moments from Postseason Baseball,
1940–1996* (1998)

Mexican Raiders in the Major Leagues

The Pasquel Brothers vs. Organized Baseball, 1946

G. RICHARD MCKELVEY

McFarland & Company, Inc., Publishers
Jefferson, North Carolina, and London

LIBRARY OF CONGRESS CATALOGUING-IN-PUBLICATION DATA

McKelvey, G. Richard, 1935–
 Mexican raiders in the major leagues : the Pasquel brothers vs. organized baseball, 1946 / G. Richard McKelvey.
  p.   cm.
 Includes bibliographical references and index.

 **ISBN-13: 978-0-7864-2563-1
 ISBN-10: 0-7864-2563-6**
 (softcover : 50# alkaline paper) ∞

 1. Liga Mexicana de Beisbol Profesional — History.
 2. Baseball — Mexico — History. 3. Baseball — United States — History. 4. Baseball players — United States. I. Title.
 GV875.L54M34   2006
 796.357'640972 — dc22   2006014354

British Library cataloguing data are available

©2006 G. Richard McKelvey. All rights reserved

No part of this book may be reproduced or transmitted in any form or by any means, electronic or mechanical, including photocopying or recording, or by any information storage and retrieval system, without permission in writing from the publisher.

Cover image ©2006 Image Club

Manufactured in the United States of America

*McFarland & Company, Inc., Publishers
 Box 611, Jefferson, North Carolina 28640
  www.mcfarlandpub.com*

Table of Contents

Preface   1

Introduction   5

1 ♦ Baseball Greets Change and War   9

2 ♦ Player-Management Issues Greet Baseball Along with the Returning Servicemen   25

3 ♦ The Mexican League: Its History and Its Dream   41

4 ♦ The Pasquels Move on Organized Baseball   57

5 ♦ Life as a Player in the Mexican League   73

6 ♦ Danny Gardella: The Pasquels' First Catch   85

7 ♦ Vernon Stephens: A Very Short Sojourn South   95

8 ♦ Luis Olmo: A Valuable Dodger Leaves Ebbets Field   103

9 ♦ Arnold Malcom "Mickey" Owen: Back and Forth to Mexico   109

10 ♦ George Hausmann, Sal Maglie, and Roy Zimmerman: Three More Giants Head South   125

11 ♦ Lou Klein, Max Lanier, and Fred Martin: The St. Louis Cardinal Jumpers   133

12 ♦ Charlie Mead, Napoleon Reyes, and Adrian Zabala: The Pasquels Strike the Giants Again   145

Table of Contents

13 ♦	Ace Adams and Harry Feldman: Two Giants Pitchers Go to Mexico	149
14 ♦	Alex Carrasquel and Roberto Ortiz: Two Washington Senators Find a Place in Mexico	155
15 ♦	Bobby Estalella, Myron Hayworth, and Rene Monteagudo: Three Pasquel Pickups	161
16 ♦	Moe Franklin, Roland Gladu, and James Steiner: They Saw Brighter Futures in Mexico	165
17 ♦	The Mexican League in 1947 and Beyond	167
18 ♦	Two More Suits	177
19 ♦	After the Return	189
Chapter Notes		195
Bibliography		199
Index		201

Preface

As a result of some of my earlier research and writings, I became aware that the 1946 baseball season was a pivotal time in the game's history. World War II was over, peace was at hand, and baseball fans were ready for an exciting season.

During the war, the military services had called many major leaguers into their ranks, and that reduced teams in the American and National Leagues to having player rosters that lacked the quality of on-the-field performers that fans had been accustomed to watching. Many wartime players were much less accomplished than their predecessors had been, and the game struggled from this and other war-related causes from 1942 through 1945.

There had been a brief period in early 1942 when some baseball administrators wondered whether or not to forgo the upcoming seasons until the war was over. President Franklin Delano Roosevelt believed that baseball offered a helpful outlet for the people of the country, and he gave a hearty "go-ahead" for the game to be played in 1942 and beyond.

When I began to focus my research on the 1946 season, I soon became aware that the growing enthusiasm about postwar baseball met some unexpected forces that were vying for the attention of the clubs' players and the teams' owners and administrators.

One of those forces was the Pasquels, who were trying to lure major league players away from their clubs to join them in the Mexican League, their major league south of the border.

With the ranks of spring training camps swollen by returning ex-servicemen, the five Mexican brothers found some players who were willing to accept their invitation and break their contracts with their teams. The Pasquels had an ample supply of money to further whet the interests of the "poorly paid peons" who were laboring north of the border.

Many of those who were the most receptive to the Pasquels' interventions were those who were caught in the numbers game that spring that had been created by the large number of returning players. They did not hold out much hope of having a significant place on their club's rosters in 1946. The Pasquels were also interested in signing some of baseball's top players and having them leave their major league teams. They offered significant amounts of money to Hank Greenberg, Bob Feller, Stan Musial, Ted Williams and others, but none took the bait.

With a growing interest in this unexpected development, I headed to the microfilm collection of the *New York Times* that was available to me in the school library where I work. This story was new to me since I was only 11 years old when it was happening.

I searched the sports pages that reported on the 1946 season, looking for mention of the Pasquels and the players who they were approaching. I discovered enough material to encourage me to search for other stories and accounts of the "Mexican Raiders." I found additional information in that summer's issues of *Time* and *Newsweek*.

I put together a bibliography of accounts of the Pasquels' incursions into the major leagues, the reactions of some of the clubs' owners, and the responses of players who saw dollar signs and new opportunities awaiting them in the Mexican League. Internet sites were helpful with information from a Mexican perspective. Accounts about the Pasquels, the history of the Mexican League, the playing conditions in Mexico, and the players on the field were available on Internet sites.

I was examining events that happened nearly 60 years ago, and I soon realized that many of my most valued resources were no longer available. In my previous writings, I had been able to draw upon the stories and accounts of events from some of those who had been involved at the time. Unfortunately, I was too late in starting this research, and I was only able to speak with a couple of people who had been part of the story in 1946 and beyond.

Preface

    The story of the Mexican Raiders didn't conclude at the end of the 1946 season. It continued for some time, as several players who had been banned from professional baseball worked through the courts to return to major league baseball. Others played in Mexico, Canada, and other countries as they continued their careers.

    The 1946 season was an exciting one. The St. Louis Cardinals nipped the Red Sox in a thrilling seven-game World Series. The game also battled an unexpected and financially potent force from Mexico that attempted to thrust its dreams and desires on some of those who played the game.

Introduction

Those connected with major league baseball — owners, administrators, managers, coaches, players and fans — looked forward to the 1946 season with renewed excitement and expectation. Baseball had experienced a downward slide during the previous two decades that had been caused by events at home and in foreign lands. The Great Depression, with the resultant financial struggles for many throughout the United States, had caused a decrease in the number of spectators in the major and minor leagues in the early part of the 1930s. World War II, which had taken players from playing fields and sent them to battlefields, had brought declining attendance, decreasing finances, and a lesser quality of major league baseball in much of the first half on the 1940s.

World War II had come to an end by 1946. However, instead of organized baseball rolling smoothly through the highly anticipated first postwar season, there were some unexpected bumps and detours along the way. First, a player-management relations dispute drew attention away from the field of play. Also, the Mexican Raiders appeared on the scene and enticed some major leaguers to pack up their bats and gloves and take them south of the border.

Early in 1946, Boston labor lawyer and baseball fan Robert Francis Murphy began to organize the American Baseball Guild (A.B.G.) that sought to help major leaguers obtain improved working conditions. Several teams formed A.B.G. chapters, player representatives were elected from those teams, and the subjects of higher salaries and an increased pension and benefits plan were central to the new organization's agenda.

Introduction

On June 4, 1946, Murphy said that a majority of players on six teams had enrolled in the A.B.G., and those on the Detroit Tigers, Boston Red Sox, and the New York Yankees were proving to be the toughest to attract.

Murphy's goals included a $6,500 minimum salary, reimbursement to the player of half of the sale price paid by another team for him, a formal grievance procedure, pension benefits, the ending of the reserve clause, and increased allowances for spring training expenses. The A.B.G. mentioned a strike as a potential offensive weapon in any war against the owners.

While the A.B.G. and the issue of players' rights and owners' responsibilities were swirling around major league baseball in 1946, the players took their places on the field, the owners tried to run their clubs as they had done in the past, and the fans welcomed back their military, ball-playing heroes who had been away from the game for some time.

The A.B.G.'s challenges to management were played out at negotiating tables while the game was in full swing.

Another force struck as the teams were preparing to open spring training camps. Five Mexican brothers, with wads of money, were making overtures to players to join their league. These Mexican Raiders had an exciting, but perhaps unrealistic, vision for baseball in their homeland.

The goal of the five Pasquel brothers — Alfonso, Bernardo, Gerardo, Jorge, and Mario — was to use the money and promises of stardom to entice major leaguers, who were under the strong arm of major league management, to leave their teams in the American and National Leagues and go to Mexico and play in their "major league." Some minor leaguers were also enticed into what appeared to be an appealing opportunity.

The New York Giants' Danny Gardella was the first player to jump to Mexico. The journeyman outfielder, who was 26 years old in 1946, had played only two wartime seasons for the Giants before being approached by the Pasquels. Vern Stephens, who was 25, had been with the St. Louis Browns since late in the 1941 season. He had been an All-Star shortstop twice and had led the American League in home

Introduction

runs with 24 in 1945. Gardella was in the Mexican League for one season, and Stephens lasted only a couple of days before "escaping" and returning to the Browns. In 1946, 21 other players had a variety of experiences south of the border.

♦ 1 ♦

Baseball Greets Change and War

Baseball teams in both in the major and minor leagues had known prosperity in the 1920s. The game was under the firm hand of Kenesaw Mountain Landis, baseball's first commissioner. He had been chosen by the club owners in 1920 to "right the ship" that had been knocked off course in 1919 by the World Series scandal involving members of the Chicago "Black Sox."

Major league attendance rose from 8.6 million in 1921 to 10.3 million in 1930. One reason was that games were now being played on Sundays. Sunday baseball had been legalized in all the states with major league clubs except Pennsylvania.

The Great Depression then delivered austerity to the nation and a financial blow to baseball's owners and players. It depleted the fans' wallets and pocketbooks, and the major league clubs were losing money as fewer fans were making their way to the ballparks. Major league attendance fell to 8.5 million in 1931, a loss of nearly two million people attending games from the previous season. Attendance plummeted to 6 million two years later. The minors also experienced a drastic decline. A promising recovery began in 1935 and major league attendance rose to 9.8 million in 1940.

Player salaries, which had risen to an average of $7,500 in 1929, fell to $6,000 by 1933 as teams struggled with their financial limitations. The average salary was up to $7,300 by 1939, but it still was below what it had been a decade earlier.

Average attendance and salary figures were just that — an average.

Some clubs made out better than others. For instance, while the New York Yankees had baseball's highest average annual attendance from 1931 through 1934 with 864,000 people coming to the Stadium in the Bronx, the St. Louis Browns pulled up the rear with an average of 123,500 fans in the seats at Sportsman's Park. In 1933, only 88,000 people came to see the Browns play baseball. In 1931, the National League's Chicago Cubs welcomed more than one million fans to Wrigley Field. The Philadelphia Phillies' average of 219,000 patrons from 1931 through 1934 was the lowest in the Senior Circuit.

Tom Yawkey, the wealthy owner of the Boston Red Sox, who took control of the club in 1933, represented a small group of magnates who had the resources available to purchase quality players even in the midst of the Depression. During the lean years, Yawkey bought Lefty Grove, Jimmie Foxx, and Bing Miller from the Philadelphia Athletics, Heinie Manush from the Washington Senators, Rick Ferrell from the Browns, his brother Wes from the Cleveland Indians, and other players. Four of them — Lefty, Jimmie, Heinie and Rick — went on to become Hall of Famers.

At the other end of the spectrum, Philadelphia's National League club — the Phillies — went bankrupt, and it was purchased by Robert R.M. Carpenter, Jr., of Delaware's duPont family.

Landis also had a hand in bringing some upheaval to major league baseball. Since his election to the newly created office, Landis had been a strong leader and, at times, an arbitrary one. During his early years as the commissioner, he had solidified the integrity of baseball. However, in the latter part of the 1930s, a couple of clubs took direct hits from him when they went beyond the rules of the game as he interpreted them.

The commissioner believed that local ownership and operation of minor league clubs was in the best interest of baseball, and he did everything within his power to curb the practice of major league clubs owning farmhands. Landis thought that the depth of some minor league systems worked against those clubs' players having a fair opportunity to make it to the majors. He regarded the farm systems as evil:

1 ♦ Baseball Greets Change and War

evil not because ownership of several non-competing clubs is bad in itself—although it questionably is preferable that every club is independently owned and operated—but evil because such ownerships are operated to control great numbers of players, imperiling their essential rights.[1]

Landis' war against farm systems worked to the benefit of some minor leaguers. In 1938, under the rule that no major league club could control two teams in the same minor league, the commissioner took action against the St. Louis Cardinals' expansive minor league system that innovator Branch Rickey had developed. On March 23, Landis declared that an estimated 100 players who belonged to six midwest teams were free agents. Although the final number of players affected was fewer than that, the action had a major impact on the Cards, and the ruling sent a clear message to other clubs. Landis' investigation showed beyond a doubt that the Cedar Rapids club and its affiliates in 1936 and 1937 were merely adjuncts to the St. Louis system and that St. Louis controlled the players on two clubs in each of three Class D Leagues in 1936 and in each of four Class D Leagues in 1937.

Two years later, Landis took similar action against the Detroit Tigers. In 1940, he freed players who were in higher classifications than the Cards' farmhands had been. Four major leaguers and 87 others in Double-A and below were declared free agents. Detroit's management

Commissioner Kenesaw Mountain Landis was in firm control of baseball during his time in office (National Baseball Hall of Fame Library, Cooperstown, N.Y.).

reported that the value of the players they lost was in excess of $500,000. The commissioner felt that the Tigers were in violation of the rules, and they were using farm clubs to hide dozens of players.

Landis used the Detroit situation as an opportunity to issue new rules regarding players and minor league clubs. No longer could a player be signed to a blank contract, and a copy of the contract must be given to the player. Working agreements could only be made with the player by the team signing that player and not by other teams connected with the signing team.

The "High Commissioner" also put a variety of responses in place for those who violated the new rules. A club would be fined from $500 to $1,000 for each offense, and the officials or employees who committed the wrongdoing also would be punished for their actions.

As commissioner, Landis "worked for" the owners, but he often made decisions that benefited the players. Perhaps his intention was to create a more level playing field for all. Shortly after baseball experienced Landis's attack on a couple of major league clubs, the game became part of a much bigger battle — World War II.

In March 1941, nine months before the Japanese attack at Pearl Harbor on December 7, 1941, the Phillies' Hugh Mulcahy, who had pitched six seasons with the club, became the first major leaguer to be drafted. The Tigers' Hank Greenberg, the American League's Most Valuable Player in 1940, was drafted and entered the U.S. Army on May 7. He was discharged right before Pearl Harbor. After the Japanese attack on December 7, Greenberg volunteered and went into the Army for the second time in 1941. That was just the beginning of the long list of professional ballplayers from the major and minor leagues who headed off to serve their country on the ground, in the air, and on the seas.

By the time the 1942 season began, there were 41 American Leaguers and 20 National Leaguers in military service. The Senators had lost 13 players off their roster. Elmer Gedeon, who had played one season with the Senators in 1939, was one of two major leaguers to die in the World War II. He was killed in France on his 27th birthday in 1944. Harry O'Neill was the other major leaguer to die in the war. He had played one game for the Philadelphia Athletics in 1939. O'Neill was killed at Iwo Jima in 1945.

1 ♦ Baseball Greets Change and War

The quality of the games was diminished. The Yankees' Joe DiMaggio and Red Sox' Ted Williams had thrilled the baseball world with their memorable 1941 feats — DiMaggio with his 56-consecutive-game hitting streak and Williams with his .406 batting average — and they were both off to military duty by the following season. Bob Feller, Greenberg, Stan Musial, and others were among the top players who joined them. As of January, 1945, 5,400 of the 5,800 players who were in all levels of professional baseball at the time of the Japanese attack at Pearl Harbor were in the armed services.[2] More than 400 active major leaguers entered the armed forces during the war. Minor league talent was so scarce that only 70 teams were in operation in 1944, down from 301 in 1941.

The prospect of a few men playing a summer game while many others were fighting for their lives led some to suggest that professional baseball take a hiatus from the field of entertainment. Alva Bradley, president of the Indians, who considered canceling the 1942 season, said, "[Baseball] is too grand a game to be turned into a farce. If I can't present baseball of high quality, I'll close my park."[3]

The Cardinals' owner, Sam Breadon, was supportive of Bradley's views. He was not excited about playing the game without "real" major leaguers on the field. The Yankees' president, Ed Barrow, said that his club would field a team even if he couldn't gather together a full complement of players.

Early in January, 1942, commissioner Landis wrote to President Franklin Delano Roosevelt, asking him for help in resolving a player-shortage problem. Landis, who had been a critic of Roosevelt's policies, was pleasantly surprised to get a "green light" for the 1942 season. F.D.R. wrote in his January 15 response to Landis:

> I honestly feel that it would be best for the country to keep baseball going. There will be fewer unemployed and everybody will work longer hours and harder than ever before. And that means that they ought to have a chance for recreation and for taking their minds off their work even more than before.
>
> Baseball provides a recreation which does not last over two hours or two hours and a half, and which can be got for very little cost. And, incidentally, I hope that games can be extended

because it gives an opportunity to the day shift to see a game occasionally.

As to the players themselves, I know you agree with me that individual players who are of active military or naval age should go, without question, into the services. Even if the actual quality of the teams is lowered by the greater use of older players, this will not dampen the popularity of the sport.

Here is another way of looking at it — if 100 teams use 5,000 or 6,000 players, these players are a definite recreational asset to at least 20,000,000 of their fellow citizens — and that in my judgment is thoroughly worthwhile.[4]

Although Landis is given most of the credit for Roosevelt's decision to keep the games going, probably Senators' owner Clark Griffith was the force behind Roosevelt's "green-light letter." Landis was on the opposite political pole from Roosevelt and he had been opposed to the United States entering the war. Griffith, on the other hand, had strong ties to the president. The Washington owner labeled Roosevelt the Senators' "mascot," because he seemed to deliver the home team a win each time he appeared at the ballpark. It is likely that Griffith appealed to Roosevelt to give the majors the go-ahead for the 1942 season in an effort to boost the country's morale.

After the United States entered the war, baseball faced difficulties in a number of areas other than losing players and administrators to the military services. The realities of a wartime economy affected the conduct of the game. Transportation was seriously curtailed, and teams had to travel to play. Balls, bats, and material for uniforms were in short supply. For security reasons, night games on the east coast were prohibited in ballparks with lights until May 1944.

In preparation for the 1943 season, baseball's second wartime campaign, Landis held a January 5 meeting at Chicago's Palmer House for the owners of major league baseball's 16 clubs. The purpose of the gathering was to discuss changes in the upcoming spring training and season.

Landis wanted all spring training camps to be north of the Potomac and the Ohio Rivers and as close to home as possible. The clubs would have to prepare for the season in colder climates, but the change of training bases would cut down on travel. Fewer exhibition

1 ♦ Baseball Greets Change and War

games were on schedule, and traveling squads could include as few as 20 players.

Under the new rule, only two teams — the Browns and the Senators — received permission to practice south of the Mason-Dixon line. The Browns were encamped in Cape Girardeau, Missouri, and the Senators had their base at the University of Maryland.

In 1943, players would be greeted by a new type of spring training that would be away from the warmth of the sunny climes. The Yankees' facilities were at the high school in Asbury Park, New Jersey. Their manager commented:

> "Things will be different," Yankees manager Joe McCarthy told reporters as he prepared for the 1943 camp. The thought of sprinting on concrete and gymnasium floors — or outdoors on frozen turf — was disheartening.[5]

The Dodgers had their camp at Bear Mountain, New York, where they used the West Point fieldhouse. The players were housed at the posh Bear Mountain Inn. A baseball diamond was laid out on the spot where the Sing Sing prison stockade had stood until 30 years earlier. Thousands of broken rocks, courtesy of the hard-working Sing Sing inmates, were just below the surface of the playing fields. A luxurious 400-by-200-foot batting cage, enclosed entirely by netting, was available inside the West Point fieldhouse. However, The Dodgers could work out indoors only when it was not being used by the cadets. The major leaguers were second-class citizens, and the available hours for playing in the fieldhouse were usually early in the morning or in the evening.

The Red Sox set up camp at Tufts College in Medford, Massachusetts, and the Boston Braves trained at the Choate School, a boys' preparatory school in Wallingford, Connecticut. The New York Giants headed for a former Rockefeller estate in Lakewood, New Jersey, and they practiced on the fairways of the golf course that was there. Other teams found practice space at similar sites.

Others besides players joined the war effort. Hank Gowdy had enlisted in World War I and, when the country entered World War II, he left his position as a coach for the Cincinnati Reds and joined the Army again, at age 53.

Mexican Raiders in the Major Leagues

Leland Stanford (Larry) MacPhail, who was a top baseball administrator, also took a furlough from the game. The charismatic and innovative president of the Brooklyn Dodgers headed off to war following the 1942 campaign. MacPhail had come to the hapless Dodgers [aka: Bums] in 1939 after having served as the Reds' general manager since December, 1933.

MacPhail improved all aspects of the Dodgers' operation, from the appearance of Ebbets Field to the excitement in the ballpark to the quality of the team on the field. The excitement was built on success rather than on the comedy that earlier had greeted the people of Flatbush when they came to the games. For many years, some form of comic relief was the most interesting thing that happened on the field. The Flatbush fans who had dodged the trolleys that ran by the stadium — these "trolley-dodgers" were the source of the club's name — were used to watching ineptitude in action. Now, with the club under the leadership of the inventive, charismatic, and provocative MacPhail, they were seeing quality.

The Dodgers climbed to the top of the National League in 1941 and went on to meet New York in the Fall Classic. The series went to the Yankees, 4 games to 1. In 1942, Brooklyn battled St. Louis in a close National League race before finishing two games behind the Cardinals.

MacPhail had served in World War I and had risen from the rank of private to captain in the U.S. Army. On October 1, 1942, Lt. Col. MacPhail began his second tour of duty as an aide to Undersecretary of War Robert Patterson in Washington, D.C.

At the conclusion of the war, MacPhail reentered baseball as a part-owner of the Yankees along with Daniel R. Topping and Del E. Webb. He also became the club's president, succeeding Edward G. Barrow.

Some players were in the Special Services during the war. Their primary duty was to play baseball to entertain the troops. Army private DiMaggio was playing ball at Camp Santa Ana, California. The Giants' Johnny Mize played first base at the Great Lakes Naval Training Station while the Cardinals' Johnny Beazley was pitching for an Army Air Corps team. The Red Sox' Dom DiMaggio and Yankees' shortstop Phil Rizzuto were both on the Norfolk Naval Training

1 ♦ Baseball Greets Change and War

Station club. Gary Bodie, the manager of the Naval Training Station team, had his pick between Rizzuto and Dodgers' shortstop Pee Wee Reese. Bodie kept Rizzuto and sent Reese a short distance down the road to the Norfolk Naval Air Station, where he joined Dodger teammate Hugh Casey. Brooklyn's Pete Reiser was at Fort Riley, Kansas.

Players in the military services played in a number of war-benefit games. On July 7, 1942, 62,094 fans filed into Cleveland's Municipal Stadium to watch the American League All-Stars defeat the Service All-Stars, 5–0. A year later, the Norfolk Naval Training Station team defeated the Senators, 4–3, in a benefit game played at Washington's Griffith Stadium. That same year, the Norfolk Naval Training Station team and the Norfolk Naval Air Station club played a seven-game set with a World Series atmosphere, which the Training Station won, four games to three.

Other major leaguers, however, served on the battle lines in the European and Pacific theaters. Cleveland's Feller, who spent 44 months in the Navy, was on the Battleship *Atlanta* in the Pacific, and Williams enlisted in the Marines and became a fighter pilot.

The Braves' Warren Spahn saw combat in Europe. The 21-year-old left-hander, who had relieved in four games with the Braves in 1942, enlisted in the Army on December 10, 1942. He narrowly missed being killed at the Ludendorff Bridge in Remagen, Germany. On March 7, 1945, shortly after walking off the bridge, the army engineer heard a blast and watched the span fall in pieces into the Rhine River. Spahn attempted to rescue some of his fellow soldiers, and, as a result of his bravery, he became the only major league ballplayer to receive a battlefield commission to the rank of 2nd Lieutenant.

Spahn recalled his wartime experiences:

> Surviving in combat is a grueling experience. At one point in 1944, I was on the line for 30 straight days... For 30 days, no shower, no change of uniform, no nothing. But we did survive on K-rations.
>
> Those military experiences helped me as a ballplayer. If I was not afraid to go into the field of battle, why should I be afraid to face a big-league hitter?[6]

Mexican Raiders in the Major Leagues

Gedeon was the only major leaguer to be killed on the field of battle. However, several other players were injured either physically or psychologically — or both — as a result of their wartime service.

Lou Brissie was one of them. In 1943, after turning 19, Brissie had a successful tryout before the watchful eyes of legendary Athletics' manager Connie Mack, who called the young left-handed pitcher "the next Lefty Grove." Brissie joined the U.S. Army rather than the A's.

On December 7, 1944, at 11:20 a.m., Brissie suffered an injury that came close to ending his life. Corporal Brissie and his men from the 351st Infantry, 88th Division, were in a truck making their way through mountains in northern Italy when Germans launched an artillery attack. Brissie yelled to his men to take cover. When the shells exploded, nine of his men were killed instantly. Only three survived. A powerful 170-mm artillery shell exploded near Brissie's feet. Brissie's left leg was shattered and bones in his feet and ankles were broken. An account of what happened next indicates the critical nature of the situation:

> He clawed along the snow-covered ground, then collapsed in a creek bed. He lay motionless for six hours, blood trickling from his mouth and ears, given up for dead by the passing corpsmen. Finally, in the fading light, someone leaned over him and found that he was breathing.[7]

Dr. Wilbur Brubaker, who treated Brissie, described the injuries and the early treatment:

> On December 7, 1944, Leland Brissie, at age 20, sustained multiple injuries yielding severe compound fractures of the left leg. On transport to each of two regional American U.S. hospitals where in each instance admittance would mean amputation of his left leg. Refusal to submit to amputation, Brissie was transported to the 300th General Army Hospital in Naples, Italy. Five days prior to Brissie's admission, the 300th General Hospital was in receipt of ample supplies of penicillin. The use of penicillin in Brissie's case was uncomplicated and after surgical removal of several parcels of fractured bone and the renewal of plaster cast support, he was returned to the U.S. for further treatment.[8]

1 ♦ Baseball Greets Change and War

Brubaker said, "As of this date, Lou Brissie represents the first successful use of penicillin protection of (from) infection in compound fractures in the prevention of amputation."[9]

After 23 surgeries to remove splintered bone and shrapnel, Brissie arrived home with both legs in casts. His left leg had been saved, but infection was an ongoing fear. Osteomyelitis, an infection of the bone, was a present and future danger. The penicillin treatments would continue and would have to be renewed at various times later in his life. The prognosis for a baseball career was poor. However, the courageous left-hander worked hard on his recovery and the hard-throwing southpaw returned to baseball with Savannah of the Sally League in 1947. He went 23–5 and set a league strikeout record, fanning 278 batters. At the end of season he made it to the Athletics to begin his major league career.

From 1942 through 1945, the teams consisted of players who were often not of major league caliber. Some of the smaller minor leagues suspended operations because of a shortage of players.

Those who had not gone to war because of age, physical disabilities, or other reasons for deferment were on the field for the 16 major league clubs. Many teams held tryout camps and hired players out of them to bolster their minor league rosters. The Cardinals, who, before the war, had one of the deepest farm systems in baseball, lost more than 250 of their minor leaguers to military service and were forced to distribute flyers advertising spots on their teams.

Some old timers came back for appearances with major league clubs. Babe Herman, who had been out of baseball since 1937, hooked on with the Dodgers in 1945, at age 42, and played in 37 games. Brooklyn also brought back 44-year-old retired catcher Clyde Sukeforth that season. He appeared in 18 games, catching in 13 of them.

Not everyone who wanted to serve could go to war. The Tigers' left-handed pitcher Hal Newhouser enlisted in the Air Force with the goal of becoming a pilot, and he planned to be inducted into military service while standing on the mound at Detroit's Briggs Stadium. Newhouser failed his pre-induction physical exam because of a heart problem that he never knew he had, and he was classified 4-F. He could not serve, but he was able to pitch for the Tigers during the war years.

After two eight-win seasons in 1942 and 1943, Newhouser rose to the top of the major leagues' pitching charts the following two campaigns. He was 29-9 in 1944 and went 25-9 in 1945. The Tigers were the World Champions in 1945 with a four games to three win over the Cubs. The Detroit lefty went 2-1 during the World Series, including the clinching victory in the seventh game.

Not all fans understood why Newhouser was on the playing field rather than on the battlefield. He remembered some of the anger that was expressed toward him:

> You got flak from people... Our friends and other people were being killed or hurt over there and we were out playing ball. I got letters from some of the veterans... One day I got a banner. The letters were about an inch wide. It was colored in yellow and the word was put in there: "BASTARD." You got a few of those things.[10]

The shortage of ballplayers provided an opportunity for two players to reach the majors — an opportunity they probably would not otherwise have had. The Browns added outfielder Pete Gray, who had lost his right arm in an accident as a child, to their roster for the 1945 season. St. Louis had picked him up from Memphis of the Southern Association. Gray played in 77 games for the Browns in his one major league season, hitting .218. He expected that the return of players who had been away at war would make it very difficult for him to find a spot on a major league roster in 1946.

In 1945, the Senators, who were searching for pitching help, signed war veteran Bert Shepard to be a left-handed hurler and a coach on the club. Shepard, a pilot of a P-38, had been shot down in Germany in May, 1944. He had to have his right leg amputated below the knee as a result of the injuries. The 25-year-old hurler wore an artificial leg to the mound for his only official major league appearance for the Senators in 1945.

On June 10, 1944, the Reds rushed 15-year-old, left-handed pitcher Joe Nuxhall to the majors, but he only lasted ⅔ of an inning before heading to the minors. Eddie Basinski, who was more talented as a concert violinist than as a baseball player, jumped from the

1 ♦ Baseball Greets Change and War

sandlots to the majors when he joined the Dodgers as an infielder in 1944.

Because of the quality of the players and the games, many fans stayed away from the ballparks. Attendance dropped from the over 9.6 million during the exciting 1941 season to 8.5 million the following summer. Only 7.4 million fans attended games in the 16 major league ballparks in 1943, the lowest it had been since 1935. In 1945, the All-Star Game was cancelled due to wartime travel restrictions. With victory achieved in Europe with the surrender of the Germans on May 7, 1945, and with the hope of ending the hostilities with Japan in the near future, attendance rose to 10,841,123. Hopefully, an upward trend in attendance was on the horizon.

From 1942–1945, the major leagues' World Championships were claimed by the Cardinals, Yankees, Cards, and Tigers in successive seasons. As a preview of the changes to come, Greenberg, whose pre-war $55,000-a-year salary had made him the game's highest-paid player, returned from military duty in July 1945. He gave Detroit a huge boost down the stretch as the Tigers battled successfully against the Senators for the American League title. He also was a key contributor to the team's World Series victory over the Cubs. Another Tiger, pitcher Virgil "Fire" Trucks, also had returned from the military, and he went to the mound near the end of the regular season. He contributed a vital win in the second game of the Fall Classic.

The quality of the game still was lacking, and according to Geoffrey Fisher and Ken Burns in *Baseball: An Illustrated History*, the 1945 World Series "was called the worst series in history —'the fat men against the tall men at the office picnic.'"[11]

The Indians' Feller was another early returnee, and the fire-balling right-hander was back on the mound for Cleveland in August.

World War II officially ended on September 2, 1945, when the Japanese signed a surrender agreement aboard the USS Missouri in Tokyo Bay. After peace was achieved, the 1946 campaign promised a return to the quality of pre-war baseball.

Prior to 1946 spring training, major league clubs realized that they would be overrun by those returning from the war. Teams made plans to provide opportunities for those who had played during the wartime seasons and for returning veterans. Minor league systems were expanded to meet the expected increased demand for places to play professionally. At the major league level, most of the wartime rosters were expected to be strengthened by returning players. The names on the 1946 major league lineup cards were expected to change dramatically.

The World Champion Tigers' 1945 lineup featured many players who probably would not play key roles with the club the following season — the season of the "return." A projected opening day lineup for the 1946 Tigers showed changes that were in store in Detroit. The same occurred with teams in most major league cities.

	1945 Tigers	*1946 Tigers*
First Base	Rudy York	Hank Greenberg
Second Base	Eddie Mayo	Jimmy Bloodworth
Third Base	Bob Maier	George Kell
Shortstop	Skeeter Webb	Eddie Lake
Left Field	Jimmy Outlaw	Dick Wakefield
Center Field	Roger Cramer	Hoot Evers
Right Field	Roy Cullenbine	Roy Cullenbine
Catcher	Bob Swift	Birdie Tebbets
Pitchers	Hal Newhouser	Hal Newhouser
	Dizzy Trout	Dizzy Trout
	Al Benton	Al Benton
	Stubby Overmire	Stubby Overmire
	Les Mueller	Virgil Trucks
	Jim Tobin	Fred Hutchinson

Like the 1946 Tigers, the Red Sox roster was expected to include players who were not available to the club in 1945. Of the 39 players who eventually found spots on the '46 roster, 21 had seen military duty in World War II. Players from the regular 1945 lineup such as "Indian Bob" Johnson, Johnny Lazor, Bob Garbark, Emmett O'Neill, Jim Wilson, Clem Hausmann, and Mike Ryba had been replaced by Bobby Doerr, Johnny Pesky, Williams, Dom DiMaggio, Hal Wagner, Tex Hughson, Joe Dobson, Earl Johnson, and Mickey Harris.

American League president William Harridge, who had been in the post since 1931, had caught the enthusiasm about the upcoming campaign and was expecting an outstanding 1946 season, with the return of the quality players from World War II.

1 ♦ Baseball Greets Change and War

In January, MacPhail, ever the innovator, had announced one of baseball's most ambitious schedules for spring training when he described the Yankees' plan for their returning players and for those who had been on the field during the war years. On the docket was a nine-game exhibition hop to Panama, a two-camp setup in Florida, and a dual march north after the close of the Florida camps. At the conclusion of the Florida encampment, one group of players and coaches would travel to Texas by airplane to play a series of games there. A second group would travel north, playing 22 games against the Dodgers along the way to New York.

The Dodgers announced that they would be opening their training camp on February 1 in Sanford, Florida, for close to 150 players, giving them a two-week jump on some of the other National League clubs. President Rickey of the Dodgers looked expectantly toward the new season and said that he was undertaking "the most important thing that ever happened to the Brooklyn ball club."[12]

Giants club secretary Eddie Brannick sent contracts to 48 of his club's players in mid–January. That was the largest squad of players to appear on the Giants' payroll in the team's history. Even more were expected to be added once spring training got under way on February 11.

Brannick didn't know at the time that eight of the 48 — Ace Adams, Harry Feldman, Danny Gardella, George Hausmann, Sal Maglie, Napoleon Reyes, Adrian Zabala, and Roy Zimmerman — would be playing under another contract in Mexico in 1946.

Management, players, and fans were ready for the game to resume with the excitement and stability of the pre-war years. The world was generally at peace, but soon the baseball world would not be.

◆ 2 ◆

Player-Management Issues Greet Baseball Along with the Returning Servicemen

World War II had come to an end, but, instead of Organized Baseball rolling smoothly into the much anticipated 1946 season, there were some unexpected bumps along the way. A player-management relations dispute that had bubbled to the surface a number of times in earlier years came to the fore again just as baseball was beginning to steady itself during the post-war period.

Boston labor lawyer and baseball fan Robert Francis Murphy was organizing the American Baseball Guild (A.B.G.) to help major leaguers obtain better working conditions. Murphy had been Harvard-educated and had worked for the National Labor Relations Board in Washington, D.C. Several teams formed A.B.G. chapters, player representatives were elected, and the subjects of higher salaries and an increased pension and benefit plan were discussed. Murphy's lofty goals included a $6,500 minimum salary, reimbursement of one half of a player's sale price to the player, a formal grievance procedure, pension benefits, the removal of the reserve clause, and increased allowances for spring training expenses. It was estimated that the average pay at the time for rookies coming into the league was $4,500 a year. The A.B.G. mentioned a strike as a potential weapon in the players' arsenal in any upcoming war against the owners.

Clark Griffith, a former player from 1891 through 1914 and the president of the Washington American League club since 1920, was dead set against the A.B.G.'s goals and methods. He said that the whole thing was "doomed to failure," adding, "Dickering between owners and players just has to be carried out individually. There are big differences in players' abilities, and I can't see a $40,000-a-year man refusing to play ball simply because another fellow makes $10,000."[1]

For most of its history, professional baseball had existed in an uneven balance between management and the players. Management held almost all of the power and those on the field had practically none. Management dictated the salaries that were kept at a minimal level, and they controlled both the present and future employment status of the players. The reserve clause provided a solid foundation for the relationship between the two unequal partners in the game.

With a large number of players returning from military service, management was in a position where it could pick and choose from a sizeable pool as to who would be on their major league clubs. That placed those on the field even more under the thumb of ownership than had previously been the case.

In 1877, a coal baron named William A. Hulbert became president of the National League of Professional Base Ball that had been founded a year earlier. To prevent players from switching teams, the clubs in the league secretly agreed to "reserve" five players at the end of each season. Owners were not allowed to seek the services of those five players.

Early in the 1880s, the reserve clause "officially" came into existence. The clause stated that owners had the right to renew a player's contract following each season, which meant that the player could be under contract to the same team for the rest of his playing career. The player also didn't have any say when he was traded or sold to another club.

There had been attempts by the players to form leagues in which they had control of their salaries and their destinies. In 1890, the eight-team Players League was formed, and it offered players an opportunity to play for pay without a reserve clause. However, the league only lasted for a single season.

Players also had tried to form a group that would be able to wield power in their relationship with management. On October 22, 1885, after citing a string of complaints about their working conditions, nine members of the New York Giants rallied behind one of their own, John Montgomery Ward, and formed the Brotherhood of Professional Base Ball Players.

Negotiations between the Brotherhood and the owners failed to produce the desired results, at least on the part of the players. The talks broke down when the owners refused to budge on key issues including "the unwritten reserve clause, unreasonable fines, and the sale of players from one club to another."[2]

There had been another attempt to bring players together to address their common concerns and to form a group that would bring some force to bear in their relations with management. On August 12, 1912, an article in the *New York Times* reported that a union of baseball players had been formed at a secret meeting in the office of David Fultz, a former outfielder for Philadelphia and Baltimore of the National League and Philadelphia and the New York Highlanders of the American League from 1898 until his retirement in 1905.

Fultz was not ready to say much about the new organization — The Baseball Players' Fraternity. After news of the organization leaked out, he said:

> This will be an association ... but will have no trade union features. The aims and objectives of the body will be to have a better understanding among all the members of the baseball clubs and the club owners, and, in short, to systemize the playing of baseball.[3]

The organization claimed to have 286 members — almost all the players in the two major leagues. A number of managers expressed an interest in joining, but Fultz said that would not happen because it might put them in an untenable position between the players and the owners.

The Baseball Players' Fraternity was incorporated in the State of New York on September 6, 1912. In the announcement of the incorporation, Fultz, who had been named the fraternity's president, mentioned several cases which indicated that players needed representation through such an organization.

He spoke about a player who had been released from a major

league team to a minor league club without passing through waivers. Fultz said that two other major league teams were interested in signing him to a contract for the same amount he was currently earning, but he was "railroaded" to the minors for a salary below his major league contract.

Fultz noted that another player was signed a three-year contract for 1911, 1912, and 1913 for $4,000 per season. In July, the player had been sold to a minor league club and was being paid $2,000 per season. The organization's president mentioned others who had been sold to the minor leagues and were also suffering financially as a result of their demotions.

Fultz outlined some of the purposes of the new organization:

> To have every reasonable obligation of the player's contract lived up to by both contracting parties. To secure adequate protection from abusive spectators.... To be of financial assistance to deserving ballplayers. To advise the player concerning any real or fancied grievance, and, in the event the former exists, to prepare his case for him.[4]

The Federal League, which began operation in 1914 and offered players more control over their salaries and working conditions, did raise concern at the time for some of baseball's powerful executives. It promised to be in competition with the existing National and American Leagues, and would offer its players an opportunity to disregard the reserve clause and find employment with clubs in the new league.

On December 29, 1913, August Herrmann, chairman of the National Commission, which was professional baseball's major decision-making body, expressed concern about plans that were being made for the start of the Federal League in the upcoming season:

> Heretofore not a great deal of attention has been paid to the new league officially by the commission. It is the general impression now, however, that more attention will be given to the new organization by the National Commission.[5]

The Federal League had some wealthy individuals who were prepared to go to war against the American and National Leagues (Organized Baseball). Jim Gilmore was a coal and paper magnate, Charles

Weeghman owned a string of lunchrooms and billiard halls in the Chicago area, Phil D. Ball was in the ice business in St. Louis, Bob Ward owned bakeries, and Harry Sinclair was an oil magnate. On the same day that Herrmann expressed his concern about a possible new league, it was announced that infielder Joe Tinker and pitcher Mordecai Brown had signed contracts with teams in that league — Tinker with Chicago and Brown with St. Louis.

Before Tinker was traded to the Brooklyn Superbas following the 1913 season, he had been the Chicago Cubs' legendary shortstop since 1902, and, was also their manager during his final season with the team.

Tinker reportedly signed a three-year, $36,000 contract with the Federal League's Chicago Whales. Weeghman was providing the major money for the new club. Tinker's salary had been guaranteed by a bonding company which meant that Joe would receive his money regardless of the league's fate.

John Heydler, the National League's secretary, appeared confused as to why Tinker would have accepted Weeghman's offer:

> The fact that Tinker would positively receive a $10,000 [bonus] for signing with Brooklyn makes the report of his jump appear all the more improbable to me, because no ball player would turn down such a large bonus for an uncertain proposition.[6]

Brown had played for the St. Louis team in the National League during his rookie year in 1903, had spent nine seasons with the Cubs, and was then traded to the Cincinnati Reds for the 1913 campaign. He had won 20 or more games six times with Chicago.

The impending competition with the Federal League, which had created a plague of player pirating and contract jumping, drove the owners and the Baseball Players' Fraternity to the bargaining table. On January 6, 1914, at a meeting in Cincinnati between the National Commission and the Baseball Players' Fraternity, the players' requests, which first had surfaced the previous September, were discussed and acted upon. There were 17 requests in all and, when all was said and done, the players had made major gains with regard to a player's freedom after no team claimed him off waivers or after he was given his unconditional release after ten years of service.

Mexican Raiders in the Major Leagues

As a result of the changes, many players in Organized Baseball had to sign new contracts in place of the ones they already had agreed to for the 1914 season.

Harry N. Hempstead, president of the Giants, was pleased with the results of the talks. He said that a great misunderstanding between the two sides had been averted.

At the end of January, the Superbas made a last-ditch effort to retain Tinker. Earlier, they had offered a $10,00 bonus and a $5,000 salary, which was the same annual pay he had received while he was with the Cubs. Brooklyn owner Charles Ebbets sweetened the pot, offering Tinker a $7,500 salary, which was what Joe originally had asked for. However, Tinker didn't budge from his commitment to the upstart Chicago Whales.

The events resulting from the arrival of the Federal League would be experienced by another player-management clash some three decades later when the Mexican Raiders offered promising opportunities for the players of that day.

Lured by the promise of increased salaries and welcoming the opportunity to get out from under the control of the reserve clause, Brown and Tinker were among 81 American and National Leaguers and 140 minor leaguers who jumped to the Federal League, which opened operation in 1914 in eight cities. Four of the cities — Brooklyn, Chicago, Pittsburgh, and St. Louis — also had teams in the major leagues. The other clubs in the eight-team league were in Baltimore, Buffalo, Indianapolis, and Kansas City.

The players' movements to teams in the Federal League resulted in a round of court cases. One of the most celebrated involved Philadelphia Phillies' catcher Bill Killefer. Killefer had played for the St. Louis Browns in 1909 and 1910. He then went to the Phillies and was with them through the 1913 campaign, when he was in 120 games and batted .244. Killefer signed with the Federal League's Chicago Whales on January 8 for three years at a total salary of $17,500, which was a substantial pay increase for him.

Twelve days after signing with the Whales, the Phillies offered him more money to return to Philadelphia and he accepted their offer. On March 20, the Federal League club brought suit in the United

States District Court in Grand Rapids, Michigan, which was the jurisdiction in which Killefer resided. They were seeking an injunction to restrain the catcher from returning to the Philadelphia team.

On April 10, Federal Judge Clarence W. Sessions denied the application for an injunction although he ruled that the reserve clause was invalid and unenforceable. He said:

> The leading authorities, with possibly one exception, are agreed that executory contracts of this nature can neither be enforced in equity nor form the basis of an action at law to recover damages for their breach. The reasons for the decisions are that such contracts are lacking in the necessary qualities of definiteness, certainty, and mutuality.[7]

Sessions said that Killefer's 1913 contract, relative to his reservation for the 1914 season, was lacking in all of these essential elements. His ruling was based primarily on his belief that the Federal League club had not come to court with "clean hands." He noted that the plaintiff was well aware that Killefer was under a moral obligation, if not a legal one, to play with Philadelphia when he was induced to repudiate his obligation and sign with Chicago. Sessions said, "In so doing, a willful wrong was done to the Philadelphia club, which was none the less grievous and harmful because the injured party could not obtain legal redress."[8]

The Federal League club appealed the ruling in the United States Circuit Court of Appeals in Cincinnati, but that court supported Sessions' decision. Killefer returned to Philadelphia and played for the Phillies.

The victory in the case involving Killefer had gone to the National League. Another decision would go the other way. Hal Chase began the 1914 campaign with the Chicago White Sox. He had played with New York of the Junior Circuit from 1905 until 1913 and had managed them for a year and a half. He was traded to Chicago early in the 1913 season and played 58 games with the team the following year. Because Chicago could release him by giving him a ten-day notice, Chase decided to give them a ten-day notice that he was leaving. At that point, he signed with the Buffalo club in the Federal League. On June

Mexican Raiders in the Major Leagues

25, 1914, while he was with Buffalo, Chase was served with injunction papers which prohibited him from playing for his new club. The Federal League sought to invoke the Sherman Antitrust Act because they believed that Organized Baseball was operating in restraint of trade.

On July 21, New York State Supreme Court Judge Herbert P. Bissell, after hearing the arguments, granted the motion to vacate the injunction that restrained Chase from playing for Buffalo. Although the judge ruled that Organized Baseball did not involve interstate commerce and was not in violation of the Sherman Antitrust Act, he said that Chase could terminate the contract at any time on ten days' notice. He wrote:

> The player's contract, executed in accordance with its terms, binds him not only for the playing season of six months from April 14 to Oct. 14, but also for another season, if the plaintiff chooses to exercise its option.... His only alternative is to abandon his vocation. Can it fairly be claimed that there is mutuality in such a contract?[9]

Other players used the Federal League threat to gain a salary increase for themselves. Walter Johnson, the ace of Washington's staff, having gone 36–7 in 1913, agreed to terms with a Federal League team but returned to the Senators for the 1914 campaign after they offered him a raise.

The Federal League owners would have pulled off a monstrous coup if they could have gotten Ty Cobb in the uniform of one of their clubs. Sinclair offered the American League batting champion a three-year contract worth $100,000. He also gave Cobb a guarantee that he would receive the money even if the league folded. Cobb, who had battled Detroit president Frank Navin almost annually for what he thought was a decent working wage, did not accept Sinclair's offer. He had signed a $12,000 contract with the Tigers and, of all people, believed that he should honor it.

Navin, however, was not convinced that Cobb was committed to play for Detroit, and he had a terrible fear that his star outfielder might depart for a more lucrative salary. Cobb, aware of Navin's concern about losing him, played the waiting game and then took on the team's owner. Cobb eventually squeezed a new three-year, $45,000 guaranteed contract out of Navin.

Cobb was required to sign a new type of contract that the American and National Leagues had just initiated. It included a new approach to players' rights:

> Now an option contract was issued by the AL and NL by which the player reserved his own services to his team for the following season, and paid for the reservation out of his salary. By signing, the player tacitly agreed to put himself on option (the club's option, not his), and so rendered the courts unable to act. As smooth as goose grease was this agreement, and few players understood the number of rights they signed away.[10]

The Federal League's Indianapolis club took the first season's pennant with an 88–65 record and 1½ game advantage over Chicago. The teams' owners, by and large, suffered significant financial losses over the course of the campaign, but the season had been played and the war had been waged.

Early in the off-season, there were some signs that the outlaw league and Organized Baseball were trying to reach an agreement before the start of the next campaign. The talks broke down when it appeared to the Federal League's leaders that the other two circuits would not recognize them officially as a third major league.

Relations were further strained when, on January 5, 1915, the Federal League's owners filed an antitrust suit in Chicago against Organized Baseball. They knew that Federal Judge Kenesaw Mountain Landis had the reputation of ruling against antitrust practices, and they asked him to rule that the reserve clause and blacklisting practices as provided for by the National Agreement be declared illegal.

Less than two weeks later, the suit was expanded to include individual players in the Federal League and the league itself. The court was asked specifically to adjudicate the relationship that a player has to Organized Baseball:

> The contracts signed by players in organized baseball were cited, and the court was asked to determine whether the agreements and their interpretation amount to a violation of the laws against

Mexican Raiders in the Major Leagues

enforced servitude, peonage, and the right of every citizen to enter into a free contract.[11]

Organized Baseball responded by submitting a number of affidavits to represent its position. Leaders of the leagues spoke up in support of what they had been doing, with Charles A. Comiskey, president of the Chicago White Sox, serving as one of the leading advocates. He had played as a professional, entering the game in 1876 at a salary of $70 a month. He declared that:

> he never broke a contract, and never objected to the ten-day clause in any of the contracts he had signed. He complains of the loss of Hal Chase and Ted Easterly, who left his club for the Federals, and also of the effect that Federal bidding had on the minds of other players.[12]

Heydler was seriously concerned about the Federal League's suit:

> The impression that seems to prevail in some quarters, that the Federal League attack on the National Agreement is a laughing matter, is not shared in by the gentlemen who took part in the Chicago preliminary conference. On the contrary, the action brought is considered the most serious attack made on the fundamental principles of professional baseball.[13]

The trial was completed in January 1915, but Landis did not make his ruling, and the Federal League's second season began without any change in the relationship between the three circuits. The only change in the makeup of the Federal League was that a team in Newark, New Jersey, had replaced the pennant-winning Indianapolis club.

In May another round of peace talks began. It was understood that Landis would withhold judgment until June 1 to allow the parties to reach a peaceful out-of-court settlement. On June 1, there was no peace and, through the summer months, there was no ruling.

In July, the Federal League began to talk about further player raids on teams in the other two leagues. Ban Johnson, the American League president and a member of the National Commission, was convinced that the Federal League could not succeed financially for much longer. He also believed that players in Organized Baseball wouldn't be foolish enough to accept the outlaw league's offers. He was, nevertheless, furious about the Federal League's plans:

> The Federal League is doing exactly what it asked Judge Landis to prevent. They went into court praying that organized baseball be enjoined from interfering with the players and business of the Federal League. Now, without waiting for the decision of Judge Landis, they announce that they are going out to get players from our leagues, regardless of contracts.[14]

At the conclusion of the 1915 season, a new round of discussions began, and, on October 2, Landis announced another delay in his decision at least until December. Additional filings had been added to the considerations regarding the case, the most recent of which was a suit brought by the Philadelphia National League club against the Whales and Weeghman, the team's president.

The discussions went into December, with charges and countercharges flying between the warring factions. Organized Baseball wanted the Federal League to withdraw its suit as a condition for peace. The outlaw league wanted to see signs that it was being taken seriously by the other side.

On December 22, peace was achieved. The Federal League disbanded and Weeghman and Ball, owners of the Chicago and St. Louis franchises, became owners of the National League clubs in their cities. With Weeghman came the Whales' ballyard, Weeghman Park, which later would be renamed Wrigley Field. The historic home of the Chicago Cubs stands today as the last vestige of the Federal League.

The owners of the Baltimore Federal League franchise were enraged by what had transpired. They wanted to buy an existing American or National League club and move it to Baltimore. When that didn't happen, the owners raised the money necessary to file a suit based on the Sherman Antitrust Act against Organized Baseball and the Federal League, which they believed had sold them out.

The core of the Sherman Antitrust Act was contained in the following three sections of the suit:

> Section 1... Every contract, combination in the form of trust or otherwise, or conspiracy, in restraint of trade or commerce among the several States, or with foreign nations, is hereby declared to be illegal....

Mexican Raiders in the Major Leagues

> Section 2... Every person who shall monopolize, or attempt to monopolize, or combine or conspire with any other person or persons, to monopolize any part of the trade or commerce among the several States, or with foreign nations, shall be deemed guilty of a misdemeanor....
>
> Section 3... Every contract, combination in form of trust or otherwise, or conspiracy, in restraint of trade or commerce in any Territory of the United States or of the District of Columbia, or in restraint of trade or commerce between any such Territory and another, or between any such Territory or Territories and any State or States or the District of Columbia, or with foreign nations, or between the District of Columbia and any State or States or foreign nations, is declared illegal.[15]

Testimony in the case began in March 1919, and the Baltimore franchise won an award of $264,000 in damages. Organized Baseball appealed the decision. The centerpiece of its appeal was the position that baseball was not involved in interstate commerce, and was not, therefore, subject to the Sherman Antitrust Act. On December 6, 1920, the District Court of Appeals in Washington, D.C., overturned the earlier decision, ruling:

> The transportation in interstate commerce of the players and the paraphernalia used by them was but an incident to the main purpose of the appellants, namely the production of the game. It was for it they were in business — not for the purpose of transferring players, balls, and uniforms....
>
> So, here baseball is not commerce, though some of its incidents may be.[16]

The Baltimore club appealed the ruling to the United States Supreme Court. Judge Oliver Wendell Holmes, writing in 1922 for a unanimous court, reinforced the earlier opinion that baseball was not involved in interstate commerce. Holmes ruled that baseball was basically a sport, conducted in local ballparks before local fans, and was not subject to prosecution under antitrust laws. The historic decision appeared to give baseball an antitrust exemption. The ruling provided the foundation for much of baseball's operations for years to come.

2 ♦ Player-Management Issues

Major league owners continued to hold players under the power of the reserve clause. None of the upstart leagues or players' organizations had been able to wrest that power from the magnates and give it to those on the playing fields. Another attempt to change this appeared on the scene in the midst of the joyful return to post-war baseball.

On June 4, 1946, Murphy registered the A.B.G. as an independent union. At the time he said that a majority of players on six teams had enrolled in the A.B.G., and that those on the Tigers, Boston Red Sox and New York Yankees were proving to be the toughest to attract. He had begun his work with the Pittsburgh Pirates because "Pittsburgh is a highly unionized city covered by both National and State Labor Relations acts."[17]

After Pittsburgh owner John W. Galbreath refused to meet with him and a committee of players to discuss working conditions with the club, Murphy called for the Pirates to strike before a June night game at Forbes Field. Commissioner A. B. "Happy" Chandler got wind of the proposed strike from Pirates pitcher Rip Sewell. A plan was put in place to line up a team of old-timers to play in place of the regular Bucs should the strike materialize. Hall of Famer Honus Wagner, Pittsburgh's 72-year-old former superstar, was one of those on deck. Sewell was successful in convincing his teammates not to strike, and the game went on as scheduled. Chandler presented a gold watch to Sewell as a token of his appreciation.

The A.B.G. also had drawn interest from players in the Pacific Coast League. Murphy said he had not talked with anyone in that league because his time was being taken up working with the major leaguers. He said that if a majority of players on any team in the Pacific Coast League wanted to join the A.B.G., that he would help them organize.

The threat of unionization by the players helped make the magnates more willing to negotiate with their employees. It was a reminder of the forces that had been at work during the time of the Federal League and Baseball Players' Fraternity in 1914, when management and the players sat down to rewrite some of the uneven operating conditions of the game.

On July 8, 1946, the leaders of Organized Baseball set up the

Mexican Raiders in the Major Leagues

Major League Steering Committee, with the Yankees' Larry MacPhail as its chairman. National League president Ford Frick and owners Phil Wrigley of the Cubs and Sam Breadon of the Cardinals were their league's representatives. President William Harridge, MacPhail, and Boston's Tom Yawkey were the members of the committee from the Junior Circuit. Leslie M. O'Connor of the White Sox [and a former associate of Landis] joined the committee in an advisory capacity.

On July 18, in a precedent-setting move, the Steering Committee initiated the formation of a management-sponsored players' committee which was invited to bring players' concerns to the owners. Three players from each league were selected to serve as spokesmen during the meetings with the Major League Steering Committee. Cleveland's Mel Harder, Chicago's Joe Kuhel, and New York's Johnny Murphy represented the American League. The National Leaguers were St. Louis' Marty Marion, Boston's Billy Herman, and Brooklyn's Dixie Walker.

The A.B.G. and Organized Baseball had sparred with each other throughout the early months of the season that had been expected to bring back the pre-war splendor of Joe DiMaggio and his hitting streak and Ted Williams' historic .406 batting average. Instead, baseball was discovering disagreement and argument.

The two sides sat down together on August 5 in the Yankees' office to engage in a new exercise — collective bargaining. MacPhail presented the owners' need to retain the reserve clause. The players spoke about salaries, fringe benefits, and a pension plan.

By the end of August, the players had been promised a number of improvements in their working conditions under a new Uniform Player's Contract. There would be a $5,000 minimum salary (although not the higher amount the players had sought), and a pension plan. MacPhail had already inaugurated baseball's first such pension plan for the Yankees.

As a result of the negotiations, the MacPhail Committee also agreed to a 30-day release clause as opposed to the existing 10-day clause, and a $500 moving allowance in the event of a trade. The players were promised that there would be a 25 percent limit on pay cuts, and the expansion of postseason barnstorming from 10 to 30 days.

There would also be a $25 per week allowance for incidental expenses during spring training. The players called the latter "Murphy money" because they viewed it as a payoff for rejecting the A.B.G. and Murphy.

Also, a new Executive Council, which included an elected player from each league, was put in place. The players, however, were not granted another of their requests that would have been a significant coup had they gotten it — that the player receive one-half of the sale price when he was sold. The owners still retained the reserve clause. MacPhail reported that "not more than 1 percent (of the players) wanted any change" with regard to it.[18]

The major source of revenue for the players' benefits would come from national radio and television income. The players had suggested a series of interleague games as a way of raising the funds to support the agreement financially. They proposed that late in the season the first-place teams in each league play each other as a prelude to the Fall Classic. The other teams, based on the standings on July 1, would play the corresponding club from the other circuit. The proposal was rejected by those who sat on the other side of the table.

The new agreement was officially approved in December 1946, at the Major League meetings in Los Angeles. There was also an agreement made between the two major leagues and the National Association, which was the governing body for the minor leagues. It established a new bonus rule which put a $6,000 limit (reduced from $7,500) on the amount of money a major league club could pay a player as an extra reward for signing a contract. If a team signed a player and paid him a bonus in excess of the limit, it would be fined.

The players were feeling more empowered and much happier as a result of the victories they had achieved through negotiations. The A.B.G. quietly disappeared. A disappointed Murphy said, "The players have been offered an apple ... but they could have had an orchard."[19]

The owners had been forced to turn their eyes from the field of play during the much anticipated season of excitement. Another force was also affecting their gaze that season.

♦ 3 ♦

The Mexican League: Its History and Its Dream

During the 1946 campaign, while the American Baseball Guild (A.B.G.) and the issue of players' rights were swirling around major league baseball, players who had been at war returned, and the fans welcomed back their not-forgotten heroes.

While the A.B.G.'s challenge to management was played out at negotiating tables, another force was intervening in the lives of the players. That force, led by five Pasquel brothers — Alfonso, Bernardo, Girardo, Jorge, and Mario — was attempting to entice players with large sums of money and the promises of stardom to leave their clubs in the United States and go to Mexico to play baseball in their "major league."

Although not much definitive information exists, it appears that baseball might have first appeared in Mexico as early as 1847, with the possibility that the first games were played by men in the United States military during the Mexican-American War. As reported:

> In 1847, if one goes to the history books, it is during that time that the United States tries to take control and the Armed Forces are in Mexico.... During the 1840s and later, there were many places where the Americans tried to control. These dates agree with the origin of the baseball in each area. The American troops played baseball and shared with the Mexicans.[1]

There were teams that played in several cities between the 1870s and 1890s, but there wasn't an official league in operation at that time.

The official beginning of the professional Mexican League was in 1925 when it fielded five teams. That summer, a short season of play came on the scene. Don Alejandro Aguilar Reyes, who was better known by his nickname "Fray Nano," and Don Ernesto Carmona were the founders of this limited operation of organized baseball in Mexico.

Reyes, a sportswriter, had spent time in the United States, and he returned home with the idea to have a baseball league in Mexico. As noted above, baseball already existed in the country and tournaments had been held on occasion, but there weren't any organized leagues.

Reyes was the league president in 1925, during the opening season, and Carmona was the manager of the Agraria club. Four other teams — Guanajuato, El Nacional de Bixler, Mexico, and 74th Regiment of Puebla City — joined Agraria in the league that began play on the last Sunday in June.

The 74th Regiment team, under manager Jesus Valdez, began the season in Puebla City but was later moved to San Luis Potosi. After a three-game postseason playoff between the Mexico club and the 74th Regiment team, the new league crowned the 74th Regiment club as its first champion.

Many players in the league were Cuban natives and others were drawn from the United States, especially from the Negro Leagues. Some of the players on the first championship club were Oscar Martinez, Javiercito Perez, and Conrado Martinez.

The clubs played a very limited schedule in the early years, and the games were played only on the weekends. For instance, in 1930, the Comintra Tigers finished the season at the top of the league with a 19–16 record.

By the late 1930s, the Mexican League was a much more formal operation. In 1937, the league featured teams from Mexico City, Vera Cruz, and Tampico. They still played a modest schedule, but the number of games was gradually increased to 100 and there were additional cities added to the independent league.

In 1937, 74-year-old Connie Mack brought the Philadelphia Athletics to Mexico for five weeks of spring training. Records show that Mexican League teams captured two games from the Athletics. However by the end of the visit, manager Mack's club held a huge lead over their Mexican opponents. The Athletics played a series of games against

3 ♦ The Mexican League

the Mexico City Agrarians, who were the previous season's champions. On March 6, the Agrarians topped the A's, 2–1, but three days later Philadelphia blasted the Mexican club, 18–1. Necaxa and the Mexican League All-Stars were some of the other teams that faced the A's during their spring training run.

"Fray Nano" founded "the Liking," the first sports newspaper in the world, in 1930. He used the newspaper to promote the Mexican League. In 1939, he published a poll to select the league's five best players since its founding. The choices were Lucas Juarez, Antonio Dolphin, Julio Molina, Leonardo Alanis, and Fernando Striped. They would later be among the first entrants in the Mexican League Hall of Fame when it was established in March 1973.

Don Beaver Montoto was another early contributor to Mexican League baseball. The wealthy Montoto and his brother-in-law Carlos Gomez Vinals founded the Puebla Chevrolet team in 1939. The club's name was derived from the type of car that Montoto sold in his automobile dealership. Chevrolet played in the Mexican Winter League against Mount of Mercy, Leon, Guadalajara, Ciasa, Juarez, Loreto, and the Tepeyac Stoves. The Chevrolet team played three seasons in the league, capturing the championship in 1941. In 1942, the team became the Puebla club of the summer Mexican League.

The Montoto family would enter the stadium on a warm afternoon through a shady entrance and take their seats in a "theater box." They were protected from the blazing sun but, unfortunately, not from irate fans who sometimes became extremely upset when Puebla committed too many errors or showed other deficiencies on the field. In a game against Monterrey, angry Puebla fans attacked the Montotos in their box.

Jorge Pasquel became the most influential person in the development and operation of the league. The fiery Jorge, who often packed a pair of diamond-studded, pearl-handled revolvers, became synonymous with the independent Mexican League in the 1940s.

Pasquel, born in Vera Cruz on April 23, 1907, was one of five brothers who became the league's leaders. He lived in Vera Cruz with his mother and brother Mario, who was a lawyer and a graduate of Notre Dame. Jorge's father and mother were divorced. The reception area of his Vera Cruz home was graced by a large statue of Napoleon. Jorge was known to have read about 25 books about Napoleon, who appeared to be his role model and hero. Jorge also had a second home in Nuevo Laredo. His Vera Cruz home was a palace, five stories high with a gymnasium occupying one of the floors. There also was a seven-car garage on the premises. Bernardo lived in Nuevo Laredo. Brother Alfonso also lived in Nuevo Laredo, and his twin brother Girardo lived on a farm near Tower.

On July 25, 1932, Jorge married Ernestina Calles, the daughter of General Plutarco Elias Calles, the former president of Mexico. Jorge's four brothers were bachelors. His marriage to Ernestina ended in divorce. Jorge, who wore a pencil-thin mustache and kept himself in good physical shape, would be romantically linked to many of the most beautiful women in the country, including actress Maria Felix, an international film star. He was often seen in public, nattily attired, in an expensive double-breasted suit with a collection of ornate and valuable rings on his fingers.

Jorge was a charismatic, dapper, dynamic, eccentric, and wealthy man, although no one seemed to know the exact amount of money that he had garnered through his vast and diverse import and export businesses. He was certainly among the wealthiest and most powerful people in the country.

The brothers first showed their money-making prowess in a small, struggling family cigar factory business in Vera Cruz. They were soon dabbling in banks, ranches, real estate, oil drilling, and steamship lines. They also were involved in handling large quantities of liquor, cigarettes, and cigars through the business ventures. The Pasquels became Mexican agents for General Motors, and controlled most of the General Motors cars that came into Mexico. Bernardo, who was much quieter than the exuberant and outgoing Jorge, played the major role in running the family's multiple businesses.

Jorge was also a customs official, and that position added pesos to his income. It also added a degree of notoriety to his resume. On February 24, 1943, the gun-toting Pasquel shot and killed a customs agent in a pistol duel. It was later determined that he had acted in self-defense.

3 ♦ *The Mexican League*

Along with his many business ventures, Jorge was a rabid baseball fanatic. He became directly involved with the independent Mexican League when he became the owner of the Vera Cruz Blues in 1940. His first major venture to improve the quality of his team and the Mexican League was to recruit outstanding players from the Negro Leagues in the United States.

The 1940 pennant-winning Blues had six players who later would achieve Hall of Fame status in Cooperstown — James "Cool Papa" Bell, Leon Day, Ray Dandridge, Martin Dihigo, Josh Gibson, and Willie Wells. Some thought that this was the greatest collection of players ever on one Mexican League squad. The Blues also climbed to the top of the league the following season and repeated as the league's champion. By that time, Pasquel had moved the team 200 miles west to Mexico City where the Mexico City team, which he also owned, played.

Pasquel was irate when Branch Rickey, who was equally rabid about developing the St. Louis Cardinals' farm system, criticized Mexican baseball after the league signed a player who was in his system. Pasquel, who had made many trips to the United States, said:

> That hurts me, that hurts my pride, that hurts the pride of all Mexicans! If American baseball wants peace with us, I am not going to go with them, they will only obtain [it] when commissioner Chandler comes here to my office, sits in that chair and explains to us what was meant with the words about Mexico![2]

At the time, baseball fanaticism was rampant in Mexico. Groups of children played the game in vacant lots, and Pasquel was engaged in a ballpark-building program for teams in the league. Puebla Park, one of those that he had constructed, was referred to as "The Cathedral of Baseball." The excitement in and around the ballparks was described in this manner:

> The games in Mexico are really a spectacle of Gods. The fans arrive long before the players arrive. Outside the park the salesmen with their merchandise align themselves, young men with tables with which it seems to be drunk smooth; others in small carts, laborers and great trays with frying pans frying meat, frijoles, tamales, tacos, compound carnitas and cakes.

> After the game begins salesmen pass between the fans offering shrimps in tomato sauce with avocado, Chile and coriander. Also there is fried chicken. In addition to which it is sold outside, smooth drinks are sold.[3]

According to reports, Coca Cola had also made it into the country and was a favorite drink around the league. Outfield billboards displayed pictures of alcoholic products made by Seagram's, Calvert, Bacardi and other companies.

The crowds were lively, loud and noisy. Live music was played continuously in the stands with cheerleaders in colorful attire dancing on the tops of the dugouts. Bookies patrolled the stands, changing the odds and taking bets on every pitch. Some players were not above putting a few pesos down on the outcome of the game. Policemen with tear-gas guns stood and watched both the action on the field and in the stands. Fans cheered loudly for their teams and banged on drums to spur them on to victory. They also whistled their disapproval of a player or a play. Whistling was the equivalent of booing during games in the states.

Jorge Pasquel would sometimes be the final arbiter in a game or in the league's business. He could reclaim a no-hitter for a pitcher who had just missed recording a gem by overturning the official scorer's decision that a player had a hit. The "hit" became an "error" after Pasquel's intervention with the official scorer.

No one knew what to expect from the fans in the stands. In the early 1940s, the Athletics played an exhibition game against the Pittsburgh Pirates in Mexico City. Al Simmons was serving in place of Mack as the A's manager, and Frankie Frisch was the Pirates' skipper. Veteran National League umpire John "Beans" Reardon was to be behind the plate for the game.

Before the first pitch, Reardon summoned the two managers to the plate and said:

> Listen to me you mugs.... Do you see that hot-tempered bunch in the stands? They'll kill me if I make a mistake. But today I don't make any mistakes. If I hear as much as a peep out of either of you in protesting any decision I quit on the spot. I'll just walk off the field and catch the first train back to the States.[4]

3 ♦ The Mexican League

Both Simmons and Frisch kept their gripes and disagreements to themselves during the ballgame, and Reardon finished in one piece.

In 1944, Rogers Hornsby, seven years after his retirement as a major league player and manager, spent part of the season playing and managing in Mexico. He discovered what happened when someone on the field went against the wishes of those in the stands or those in an administrative capacity. For Hornsby, it was a disgruntled promoter who got in his way. According to the tale, the promoter was irate after Hornsby hit a game-winning home run as a pinch-hitter in the ninth inning of a game that won him a sizeable jackpot of money. The complaint was that Hornsby's blast ruined interest in upcoming games and would lower the attendance for those games. Hornsby quit then and there and returned to the United States. The "home run story" unfortunately doesn't hold up, according to the Mexican League's records, which show that he played in only two games with Vera Cruz, getting a walk in one of the games and banging a game-winning, three-run double in the other.[5] Maybe that double became the mighty home run in the telling of the story.

Sportswriter Dave Egan gave his opinion about Hornsby's sojourn to Mexico:

> There would be fierce resentment, I feel sure, if Man o' War were put to work pulling a vegetable wagon through his declining years, and the Society for the Prevention of Cruelty to Animals would take an immediate interest in the affair. But the baseball brethren will derive smug satisfaction from the fact that one of their immortals will play in the patched-roof circuit, and one of their idols will gather the dust of sleepy Mexican towns. He sinned against their narrow code, and as a sinner should he now get his comeuppance.[6]

By the mid–1940s, it was reported in Mexico that teams in the league were traveling comfortably by air and by train, although some of the media in the United States were saying that much less advanced and much more uncomfortable methods of transportation were the usual forms of travel.

In an attempt to improve the quality of play in the Mexican League, the Pasquels looked to the United States to find players who would be interested in playing in their country. Money was an enticing part of the invitation. Jorge Pasquel, among others, viewed the Negro Leagues in the United States as a fertile field in which to cast his pesos in the hope of bringing top players to teams in Mexico.

Because of the segregation that existed in major league baseball until Jackie Robinson joined the Brooklyn Dodgers in 1947, blacks were welcome only on Negro League clubs or on minor league teams in the Dodgers' organization just before 1947. Those blacks who probably had the ability to play at the major league level were relegated to play in surroundings and conditions that were difficult, and they earned minimal salaries:

> Life in the Negro Leagues was hard. Official league games usually numbered less than 50, but exhibition play stretched seasons to about 200 games. Players often slept and ate on the team bus, as few hotels and restaurants served Afro-Americans at the time.[7]

The Mexican League owners could offer players an appealing salary to play winter ball to supplement what they were earning in the United States, or an increased salary to play during the summer south of the border.

The opportunity to join teams in Mexico proved to be beneficial to both parties — the black players from the north and the Mexican League. Some of the best Negro League players went to play baseball in Mexico, and they often became the best players in the league.

Some of baseball's greatest black players gained playing time and pesos by taking their immense skills to the Mexican League. Members of the Hall of Fame in Cooperstown besides Bell, Dandridge, Day, Dihigo, Gibson, and Wells also included Roy Campanella, Monte Irvin, Walter "Buck" Leonard, and Satchel Paige. Other Negro Leaguers, who have not been voted into the Hall of Fame in Cooperstown, such as pitcher Theolic "Fireball" Smith and catcher Quincy Trouppe also excelled both in the United States and in Mexico. Smith, with the exception of 1943 when he was with the Cleveland Buckeyes in the Negro Leagues, played for the Mexico City team from 1940–1948, putting together a 121–90 record. Trouppe had a .304 batting average in

3 ♦ The Mexican League

eight seasons with Monterrey, Mexico City, and Jalisco. Trouppe, besides his time in the Negro Leagues and in the Mexican League also appeared in six games with the Cleveland Indians in 1952.

Smith and Trouppe were involved in a deal that illustrated Jorge Pasquel's far-reaching connections. The two players were eligible for induction into the military services in 1944, but Pasquel struck a deal with some U.S. officials to supply 60,000 Mexicans to pick cotton or work in factories for two years in exchange for giving deferments to Smith and Trouppe so that they could go to Mexico to play baseball.

James "Cool Papa" Bell also accepted the Pasquels' call. He was born in Starkville, Mississippi, on May 17, 1903. Bell played for several Negro League teams from 1922 to 1946, including the St. Louis Stars, the Pittsburgh Crawfords, the Kansas City Monarchs, and the Pittsburgh Homestead Grays.

Bell was one of the first Negro Leaguers to spend time in Mexico. In 1932, in search of more money for playing the game, he went there before joining the Crawfords a year later. He also played in the Mexican League from 1938 through 1941 where he earned $450 a month, his highest salary during his 14-year playing career. Bell played for the Tampico, Torreon, Vera Cruz, and Monterrey clubs during his seasons in Mexico.

In 1940, the fleet center fielder led the southern Mexican League with a .437 average, 119 runs scored, 167 hits, 15 triples, 12 home runs, 79 runs batted in (RBI), and a .685 slugging percentage in the 90-game season. Surprisingly, Bell, who was probably best known for his blazing speed, finished the campaign as runner-up in the stolen base race to Sam Bankhead, a fellow Negro Leaguer. Satchel Paige once described Bell's speed, saying, "He could turn off the light switch and jump into bed before the light went out."[8]

Bell finished his time in the Mexican League with a .367 average for his career south of the border.

Martin Dihigo was born in Mantanzas, Cuba, on May 24, 1905. The outstanding pitcher and hitter played from 1923 through 1950 with teams in his homeland, Venezuela, Puerto Rico, the United States, and Mexico. For more than a quarter of a century, Dihigo was the ace of many of his clubs' pitching staffs, a league leader in home runs, and

Mexican Raiders in the Major Leagues

batting average. He played every position except catcher during his career. He would become the only player, black or white, to be elected to Hall of Fames in three countries: the United States, Cuba, and Mexico.

Dihigo played in the summers of 1937–1944, 1946–1947, and 1950 in the Mexican League. He displayed his outstanding skills with a number of clubs, including Aguila, Vera Cruz, Torreon, Nuevo Laredo, and Luis Potosi. His record as a pitcher was 119–57 during his 11 seasons in Mexico. Dihigo was also the league's batting champion in 1938 with a .387 average, and he posted a .317 batting average for his Mexican League career.

Although the Mexican League had begun in 1925, it was not until 1937 that official statistics were kept. Dihigo arrived in Mexico on August 8, 1937, for his first season in the league. On September 16, while pitching for the Aguila Eagles against Nogales, he threw the league's first recorded no-hitter. He struck out 15 batters in Aguila's 4–0 victory.

His best season was 1938 when the league's batting champ went 18–2 as a pitcher with a minuscule 0.92 Earned Run Average (ERA). He registered his highest win total in 1942 when he had a 22–7 record with Torreon.

On September 5, 1938, Dihigo was matched up for the first time against another of the game's greatest hurlers, the Agrarians' Paige. Paige had come to play in the league on August 9.

The Eagles held a two-game lead over the Agrarians at the start of the three-game series between the two clubs. The outcome of the three games would go a long way in determining the season's champion. Dihigo pitched his club to a 3–1 win over Paige and the Agrarians. At the time, Paige was suffering from an arm injury that had occurred while he was playing winter baseball in Venezuela. The two ace right-handers faced each other again two weeks later. Paige was no match for Dihigo, and Aguila defeated the Agrarians, 10–3. Along with his work on the mound, Dihigo went 6-for-6 at the plate.

Dihigo was elected to the Mexican Baseball Hall of Fame in 1964.

Paige had a very brief Mexican League career. He appeared in only three games that summer, pitching 19⅓ innings. There was a story that

3 ♦ The Mexican League

Pasquel asked Paige to return the $5,000 he had given him for pitching, and when Paige refused, he had the legendary hurler beaten up. Paige soon returned to the United States to rehabilitate his arm, and he didn't play in the Mexican League again.

Willie Wells was born in Austin, Texas, on August 10, 1905. He played for a number of different teams in the Negro Leagues from 1924 through 1948, beginning with the St. Louis Stars and finishing his career with the Memphis Red Sox. As his playing career progressed, the smooth fielding and clutch-hitting shortstop also added the managerial role to his resume.

In 1940 and 1941, Wells played for Vera Cruz before moving to the Tampico club in 1943. He returned to Vera Cruz in 1944, which was his final season in the Mexican League. He batted .345 and .347 in his first two years in Mexico and finished with a .323 career average for his four seasons in Mexico. While there, the fans dubbed him "El Diablo."

Josh Gibson had a short career in the Mexican League. The talented catcher, who was born in Buena Vista, Georgia, on December 21, 1911, began his professional career in 1930 with the Homestead Grays. In 1932, he jumped to the cross-town Crawfords. Besides his work behind the plate, Gibson was also an outstanding slugger, leading the league in home runs in 1932, 1934, and 1936.

Gibson, who was known as "the Black Babe Ruth," moved back and forth from the Grays to the Crawfords and had a combined 17-year career with the two clubs. Legend has it that the prodigious slugger hit a baseball completely out of Yankee Stadium, and he won home-run titles throughout his career. He captured his first batting title in 1938, hitting .440, and he posted a career .373 batting average.

He was invited to bring his outstanding skills to the Mexican League, but he only played there in 1940 and 1941 for Vera Cruz. He batted .467 during his initial season in the loop, and he .374 his second and final year with Vera Cruz. In 1941, he slammed 33 home runs and had 124 RBI.

The Homestead Grays' owner asked the courts to force Gibson, who had reneged on his contract with the team, to return to the United States. That, combined with the fact the he became quite ill while in

Mexico, caused him to return to the United States. He resumed playing for the Grays in 1942, and he retired in 1946. He died from a brain tumor at age 35 in 1947, a few months before Jackie Robinson made it to the major leagues with the Dodgers. He was elected to the Mexican Hall of Fame in 1971.

Walter F. "Buck" Leonard was born on September 8, 1907, in Rocky Mount, North Carolina. The left-handed hitting first baseman was the backbone of the Homestead Grays in the late 1930s and 1940s. As a teammate of Gibson, he helped lead the Grays to nine consecutive Negro League championships from 1937 to 1945, and he posted a .355 lifetime batting average.

Leonard played in Mexico in the winter to supplement his salary after some of the seasons with the Grays. He began with a $125 monthly salary in the Negro Leagues for the four-and-a-half month season, but during World War II he jumped to the elite level of player and earned $1,000 a month. When the Grays disbanded in 1950, having lost players to the integrated major leagues, Leonard went to play in the summer Mexican League. He was in Mexico from 1951 through 1955, playing for Torreon from 1951 through 1953 and Durango in 1954 and 1955. He averaged .326 during his three seasons with Torreon. Leonard was 48 years old when he retired from baseball in Mexico.

After the color line was broken in the major leagues with the arrival of Jackie Robinson in 1947, Bill Veeck tried to sign Leonard to play for the Indians. Leonard, who was 40 at the time, believed that he was too old to join the Indians, although Paige already had made the step.

Ray Dandridge was another Negro League star who has been inducted into the Baseball Hall of Fame in Cooperstown, NY. Dandridge was born in Richmond, Virginia, on August 31, 1913. His professional career began in 1933 when he joined the Detroit Stars and, in between time spent in Mexico, he played in the Negro Leagues and then in the New York Giants' farm system until 1953.

In 1940, Pasquel's promise of increased salary lured Dandridge to Mexico, where he made about $10,000 a season with paid living expenses and a maid. He was not forced to live in a segregated environment and felt like a first-class citizen. The third baseman, who also played shortstop, was known as "Dandy" and "Hooks." Dandridge became a Mexican hero, hitting .331 during the eight seasons he spent south of the border.

He hit .346 in 1940 to help Vera Cruz capture the Mexican League championship. The following three seasons he hit .367, .310, and .354 with the Vera Cruz club. He didn't play in Mexico in 1944, but he returned for four more years in the league in 1945. He spent three seasons with Mexico City and another with Vera Cruz. In 1948, while with Vera Cruz, he led the league in batting with a .369 average.

In 1949, Dandridge left Mexico to manage the New York Cubans. Later, he was signed by the New York Giants and played a couple of seasons with the Triple-A Minneapolis Millers. He was named the American Association's Most Valuable Player in 1950 when he batted .311 and led the league in hits. Dandridge concluded his career in 1953 after playing in the Pacific Coast League with Sacramento and Oakland.

Dandridge was elected to the Mexican Baseball Hall of Fame in 1989.

Leon Day, a hard-throwing, 5-foot-9-inch, no-windup pitcher, dazzled Negro League hitters during a lengthy career which extended from 1934 until 1950. He was born on October 30, 1916, in Alexandria, Virginia. Day began his professional career in 1934 with the Baltimore Black Sox, and he later played for the Brooklyn Eagles, Newark Eagles, and Baltimore Elite Giants before retiring in 1950. He was considered by many to be the Negro Leagues' best pitcher, and he holds their highest winning percentage at .708.

Day also spent three summers pitching in Mexico. He was with the league champion Vera Cruz club in 1940, going 6–0. He returned to play for the Mexico City Reds in 1947 and 1948 and posted a combined 18–20 record for the two seasons. The following year, he was back in the Negro National League, helping the Elite Giants win the Negro National League pennant.

Roy Campanella was the first Negro League player who spent time playing in Mexico to make it to the major leagues. He was born on November 19, 1921, in Philadelphia, Pennsylvania, and he joined the Baltimore Elite Giants as a part-time player in 1937, although he was only 15 years old. He later played full-time for the team.

Mexican Raiders in the Major Leagues

Campanella had a short Mexican League career. After a dispute with Baltimore owner "Smiling" Tom Wilson in 1942, Campanella jumped to the Mexican League and played 20 games for Monterrey in 1942 and a full season in 1943. He hit .291 for his Mexican League career. He returned to the Elite Giants, but he was soon signed by Rickey to play for the Nashua, New Hampshire, club in the Dodgers' minor league system. He made his major league debut with the Dodgers on April 20, 1948. Campanella was elected to the Mexican Hall of Fame in 1971.

Monte Irvin was born in Columbia, Alabama, on February 25, 1919. He played with the Newark Eagles under an assumed name while he was attending Lincoln University, and he continued with the team through 1941.

After leading the Negro National League in 1941 with a .396 average, Irvin asked owner Effa Manley for a $25-a-month raise on his monthly salary of $165. When Manley refused the request, Irvin went to the Mexican League for the 1942 season. There, in 63 games, he hit .397, and slammed 20 home runs with 79 RBI for the Vera Cruz club. Irvin won the Triple Crown and was named the league's Most Valuable Player.

During his triple-crown season, Irvin and Campanella played against each other several times. Vera Cruz was trailing and had the bases loaded when Irvin came to bat late in one of the games. Jorge Pasquel yelled to Irvin that he would give him $200 dollars if he won the game. After taking a strike, Irvin told Campanella that he would split the money with him if he called for a fastball. Irvin spoke to Campanella in English so that the umpire wouldn't understand the conversation. Campanella called for a curve ball, which Irvin thought he would do. Irvin was ready for the pitch and hit a game-winning homer. When Irvin arrived at home plate, Pasquel was there with the money, and Irvin pocketed all of it as he smiled at Campanella.

Irvin was drafted into the military after the 1942 season, and he spent three years in the service. Following the war, he returned and played for Newark again until 1949 when he was signed by the New York Giants and debuted with the major league club on July 2, 1949. Irvin was elected to the Mexican Hall of Fame in 1971.

3 ♦ The Mexican League

The Mexican League had a lengthy history of improving its teams by bringing outstanding Negro Leaguers to play for its teams. The Pasquels provided much of the leadership, enthusiasm, economic resources, and business acumen to accomplish this. Following World War II, they turned their eyes to the Unites States again and sought other players to supplement their lineups. This time it was not Negro Leagues players who were the object of their search.

♦ 4 ♦

The Pasquels Move on Organized Baseball

Before the opening of the 1946 spring training camps, the Mexican League launched raids on Organized Baseball's major league talent, offering them sizeable salaries to play ball south of the border. The league, which soon became known in Organized Baseball as "the outlaw league," was independent in status, and was run and financially supported by five Mexican Pasquel brothers—Alfonso, Bernardo, Girardo, Jorge, and Mario. The rival Mexican National League was also in operation, and in 1946 it became a Class B league that was connected to Organized Baseball in the United States.

In mid–February, there were rumors that the Pasquels were planning to sign a large group of players in Organized Baseball to add to the talent in their country's "major league." Their plan had been instituted initially in 1945 when the league drew four major leaguers to Mexico to play there. The Cincinnati Reds' Tommy De La Cruz, the Washington Senators' Chile Gomez and Roberto Ortiz, and the Chicago Cubs' Chico Hernandez had all left their clubs for baseball in Mexico.

Financial resources did not appear to be any problem for the venture. The Pasquels were engaged in an import-export business and there were reports that they had at least $40 million (American) behind the Mexico City and Vera Cruz clubs that they owned. The brothers also had some control over the other six clubs in the league. The Pasquels aimed to entice "poorly paid peons" (players) in the American and National Leagues to leave their clubs for a new life in baseball

Mexican Raiders in the Major Leagues

with larger salaries and bonuses in a tax-free environment. Once Organized Baseball took serious cognizance of the new threat, it went to war against the "outlaw league."

On February 19, it was announced that Danny Gardella, a second-year outfielder with the New York Giants in 1945 and a player of modest ability, had signed a contract to play for the Vera Cruz Blues. It was reported that Pasquel had offered Gardella $8,000 with a $5,000 signing bonus, which was more than twice the salary he was making with the Giants. Gardella pondered the offer for a brief time and then accepted it.

Jorge Pasquel had met Gardella at a New York City gym and told the 25 year old that riches awaited him and other players in Mexico City, Vera Cruz, Monterrey, Tampico, Nuevo Laredo, Puebla, San Luis Potosi, and Torreon. San Luis Potosi and Torreon were the two newest members of the league, having been added the previous winter.

It was later reported that the Giants' Nap Reyes and Adrian Zabala, the Philadelphia Phillies' Rene Monteagudo, and the Philadelphia Athletics' Roberto Estalella had signed to play in Mexico.

As yet, major league owners did not take the prospect of losing some of their players very seriously. With better players returning from the battlefields to reclaim their places on the playing fields, it was anticipated that Gardella, for instance, would spend the 1946 season in the minors. The loss of Gardella, who had hit .267 in 1945 against pitching staffs that had been severely depleted by the war, was not thought to be a serious problem for the Polo Grounders. Some of the players, such as Reyes and Estalella, were from Latin American countries, and they had helped to fill out the major league rosters during the war, but they were facing the possibility of not being integral players during the first post-war season.

The owners were clearly in the driver's seat as the new campaign approached, and promises of success both on the field and in the economics of the game brought joy to their faces.

During the next couple of months, the Pasquels set their sights on and aimed their money at some of the best major leaguers. Cleveland's Bob Feller, Detroit's Hank Greenberg, St. Louis' Stan Musial, and Boston's Ted Williams were among those mentioned as possible defectors, but none of them took the offers. On March 12, it was reported that right-handed pitcher Roger Wolff, who had gone 20–10 with the Senators the previous season, had turned down a Pasquel offer of a three-year, $100,000 contract with a $15,000 signing bonus.

Johnny Pesky, who had been the Boston Red Sox' rookie shortstop in 1942 before going into military service for four years, recalled being "enticed" by an offer to leave his club in 1946. It is possible that the person who spoke to him about it was Robert Janis, who was the Pasquels' major recruiter in New York at the time. Pesky remembered:

> During our first trip to New York, I was in the hotel room when there was a knock on the door. (According to the season's schedule, the Red Sox were in New York from May 10–12. They were in the midst of a very exciting season and were 20–3 at the time.) Bobby Doerr was my roommate and I think that he was in the room at the time, but maybe not. I don't remember the man's name who was at the door. Somehow he had gotten my room number. He said that he was a representative of the Pasquels. He wanted me to jump ship and leave the Red Sox and go to play baseball in Mexico. He offered me about $45,000 to play in the Mexican League. I also think that he wanted (Ted) Williams to also go to Mexico. He may have also wanted Doerr.
>
> When they were throwing around that kind of money it was very enticing. It was much more than the $4,000 that I was making at the time. It seemed like such an unnatural thing to do, so I didn't take him up on his offer.[1]

Bobby Doerr, a member of the Hall of Fame, did not appear to be on the Pasquels' list. In a recent letter he wrote, "I just remember this happening but was never approached at all. Can't tell you anything about it."[2]

Dominic DiMaggio, who like Pesky and Doerr had returned to the Red Sox in 1946 after spending time in the military, wasn't approached by the Pasquels. He said, "I must not have been good enough for them to be interested in me. I know I wouldn't have gone had I been given the opportunity."[3] DiMaggio was "good enough" in 1946 to hit .316, and he was chosen to play in that year's All-Star Game as the American League's starting center fielder.

An offer was made to a young Brooklyn farmhand — Jackie Robin-

Johnny Pesky turned down an offer from the Pasquels and remained with the Boston Red Sox (courtesy Boston Red Sox).

son. He was approached by an agent of the league in March, who offered him $6,000 per season, plus all expenses for himself and his wife. Robinson, who was ticketed to play for the Brooklyn Dodgers' Montreal farm club in 1946, turned down the contract offer and chose to stay with the Dodgers' organization. An irate Branch Rickey, the Dodgers' president, upon learning of the agent's presence at the ballpark and his offer to Robinson, tracked him down and chased him from the premises.

The Pasquels also wanted to sign Pete Gray, the St. Louis Browns' one-armed outfielder, who had been sold to Toledo of the American Association the previous winter. Gray did not accept the offer to go to the Mexican League, and he held out hope that he would eventually be picked up by a major league club.

While spring training was moving along in the states, the Mexican League was preparing to open its 1946 season with a pair of new teams and the improved talent that had been delivered by the Pasquels. The eight teams in the league were scheduled to play three games a week — Thursday evenings, midday on Saturdays, and in the morning on Sundays in an effort to avoid the hottest part of the day. There was talk about adding a fourth game to the schedule either later in the season or in 1947. As the season progressed, the teams began playing four games a week — Thursday through Sunday.

The financial plan for the league was to have 55 percent of all receipts put in a common pot, and that money would be equally distributed to all eight teams at the conclusion of the season.

Admission to the league's games ranged from five pesos ($1) to 15 pesos ($3). The Vera Cruz and Mexico City teams both played at Delta Park in Mexico City, which is 2,480 meters (a little over 8,000 feet) high. The Vera Cruz club had been moved 200 miles west to Mexico City because it was too hot and muggy during the summer months in the team's former home. The stadium sat 22,000 people and often there were only standing room admissions available long before the start of the games. The altitude was welcoming to hitters who had power and for some who did not.

The other ballparks in the league left much to be desired in terms of playing surfaces and fan and player comforts. The largest ballpark in the league was in Tampico, with a 30,000 fan capacity, and the smallest was in Nuevo Laredo, with seating room for 7,500. Nuevo Laredo was a town with a population of only 10,000 people.

The Mexican League's opener was delayed for a few days. There were two stories as to why Jorge Pasquel had pushed back the first game. One account said that he was trying to deliver more players from Organized Baseball before the opening game was played. Another account said that the league was having difficulty obtaining major-league quality baseballs and bats because American manufacturers were refusing to sell them to the Mexican League, and Jorge Pasquel was waiting for a shipment of them to arrive.

The Mexican League finally opened its 1946 season on March 21, with Vera Cruz beating the Mexico City Reds, 12–5. With an overflow crowd of 33,000 fans crammed into Delta Park, for the first time a Mexican president, Manuel Avila Camacho, threw out the ceremonial first pitch. Fans sat in the aisles, and when they were filled, they were allowed to crowd onto the field in foul territory where they were patrolled by militiamen. Jorge Pasquel and his four brothers reveled in the excitement. A total of 700,000 fans turned out for the league's first 24 games. It was a new day for baseball in Mexico!

A new political figure took center stage in Mexico as the season progressed. Jorge Pasquel often was seen by the side of Miguel Aleman, the country's new president. He had been a major contributor to Aleman's campaign and expected to be close to the new president's operation.

Twenty-three players would spend time during the 1946 campaign south of the border. Not all who signed to play in the league were satisfied with their new lives. Vern Stephens, the St. Louis Browns' 25-year-old starting shortstop, had signed to play in Mexico, but he quickly discovered that conditions were not what he was told they would be. Stephens returned to the Browns on April 6, even though Jorge Pasquel offered him an increased salary to stay and play with Vera Cruz. Stephens negotiated a new contract with the Browns which was better than his pre–Mexico offer had been, and he played 115 games for them in 1946.

A few discussions about ways to bring about peace and understanding between the Pasquels and baseball leaders in the United States were beginning to be planned or to take place. On March 12, Bernardo Pasquel said that he was prepared to meet United States officials on the border to talk over terms of an agreement. Jorge Pasquel announced that he would accept baseball commissioner A.B. "Happy" Chandler's proposal for a United States-Cuba-Mexico baseball pact provided his league received "major league status." It was the final part of his statement about "major-league status" that was the major stumbling block.

J. Alvin Gardner, president of the Texas League, looked ahead and offered to serve as a peace ambassador following the 1946 season in an effort to bring Pasquel's Mexican League into Organized Baseball. He believed that the league could qualify for a Class AAA designation, and he saw the situation as a repeat of what had happened when Montreal and Toronto joined Organized Baseball's minor league system. Gardner believed that Jorge Pasquel would be amenable to bringing his new league under the auspices of Organized Baseball if he were approached in the right way.

A meeting between Bernardo Pasquel and Clark Griffith, the president of the Senators, was scheduled for March 17 in Havana, Cuba. Griffith and Pasquel had exchanged bitter words earlier in the week about the raids that were continuing on teams in Organized Baseball. Their meeting never took place.

The Mexican Embassy in Washington also felt the heat of the battle for players from the United States. An individual close to Ambassador Antonio Espinosa de los Monteros suggested that the owners were missing an opportunity to assist in international understanding. He noted that the Ambassador was very interested in baseball, having played it as a child and while he was a student at Gettysburg and Harvard. The Mexican official asked:

> Why all the fuss about some American players going to Mexico? It looks like a rare opportunity for baseball to go to bat in furthering the exchange of international ideals....
>
> We exchange students, professors, artists, workers and so on, so why not ball players? After all, we learned baseball from Americans.[4]

Mexican Raiders in the Major Leagues

A U.S. State Department official, who asked not to be identified, also expressed his concern about the growing antagonism between baseball officials in this country and their Mexican counterparts. He said that the controversies surrounding baseball were injuring relations between the two countries.

Ty Cobb, who had retired in 1928, expressed his opinion that the players were making a mistake by leaving for baseball in Mexico. He recalled how he had turned down a $100,000 offer in 1914 to break his contract with the Detroit Tigers to join the Federal League. He believed that breaking a contract was wrong, and he stayed in the American League for 14 more years and never regretted the decision that he made.

Some in the U.S. media were speculating that the Pasquels' funds would run out and the Mexican League would not be able to complete its season. Jorge Pasquel offered to pay the doubters their expenses to Mexico and give them tickets to the games so that they could watch the Mexican League in operation.

Jorge Pasquel was so confident in the success of his league that he offered a $2 million wager to Organized Baseball. He challenged the United States' interests to also put $2 million on the table. The $4 million would be there for either Organized Baseball or the Mexican League to collect, based on the success of the Pasquels' ventures. Jorge Pasquel believed that his league was paying a fair wage to its players whereas Organized Baseball was only willing to pay slave wages.

Pasquel said that he was seeking retaliation because of actions of Organized Baseball. He mentioned that he had been unable to buy baseballs and bats from American companies who feared reprisals from Organized Baseball if they did business with the Pasquels.

As time passed and the major leagues' season openers approached, some owners, who had been rather quiet on the sidelines, began to take the situation much more seriously. The Brooklyn Dodgers lost two players. Luis Olmo, a native of Puerto Rico and a .313 hitter with 110 RBI in 1945, and catcher Mickey Owen signed to go to Mexico. On March 31, the Giants watched as second baseman George Hausmann, pitcher Sal Maglie and rookie first baseman–outfielder Roy Zimmerman packed their bags and departed. Maglie had signed a Mexican

League contract that paid him five times more than he would have made with the Giants.

The Pasquels had plans for luring more than players to Mexico. On April 8, it was reported that they had offered Chandler a $50,000 annual salary to become the Mexican League's high commissioner. The money plus living expenses did not interest Chandler. Chandler was more interested in making sure that the players who left for Mexico would not have an easy return to Organized Baseball.

Baseball was prepared to begin the 1946 season in the United States, and excitement was in the air. On April 16, in Washington, D.C., president Harry S Truman threw out the ceremonial first pitch before the opening game between the Senators and the Red Sox. Franklin D. Roosevelt had been the last president to toss the pre-game pitch before the opener when he made his delivery in 1941. Griffith Stadium welcomed 32,300 men, women, and children for the first game of the campaign. Across the country, in eight American and National League parks, 236,730 fans passed through the gates. It was the largest attendance for the start of a season in 15 years.

Organized Baseball made its first strike at the Mexican League on Opening Day, when Commissioner Chandler announced that he had instituted an automatic five-year suspension for all of the players who had jumped their contracts to play in foreign leagues.

The commissioner had given an earlier indication that he would be taking such a stand. On March 20, at a meeting in Havana, Cuba, Chandler had said that he was considering a lengthy suspension for players who hadn't returned to their clubs by Opening Day.

At the time, Chandler was in Cuba examining what steps he would take in another matter. He was considering penalties against certain players who had played in the Cuban Winter League, contrary to what their contracts in Organized Baseball allowed. According to Chandler, there were 54 players under investigation either for playing in the Cuban League after the prescribed time limit of 10 days following the close of the major league season or 31 days after the end of the minor league season, or for playing against ineligible players.

While watching the regular season's opening game between the Reds and Cubs, Chandler announced that players who had not returned to their clubs had been suspended and would not be eligible to apply for reinstatement for five years.

The Pasquels were pleased with the opportunity that Chandler's ruling had provided for them. As they understood its ramifications, there would be no place for the players who had come to Mexico to play after the 1946 season and beyond. They thought that it would give the players who had jumped from Organized Baseball a reason to remain in Mexico for future seasons.

The attempts by "Pasquel, Pasquel & Pasquel" to lure American ballplayers to Mexico wasn't lost on the people at Braves Field to watch the opener between Boston and Brooklyn. During the opening ceremonies, a trio of musicians sporting sombreros stood in front of the visiting Dodgers' dugout and played "South of the Border." After finishing their musical rendition, they tossed fake pesos into the stands.

Earlier, the leadership of all three of the New York teams—the Dodgers, Giants and Yankees—had spoken publicly that all was well with their clubs with regard to the Mexican Raiders. However, Larry MacPhail, the president of the Yankees, became the first of the three New York presidents to ratchet up the response to baseball's growing problem. On May 4, the Yankees obtained an order from the State Supreme Court restraining agents of the Mexican Baseball League and a New York

Larry MacPhail served in the military during World War II. After his discharge from the army in 1945, he became part owner and president of the New York Yankees. He would soon be at war against the Mexican raiders (National Baseball Hall of Fame library, Cooperstown, N.Y.).

sportswriter from attempting to induce any member of the Yankees to forgo his contract and leave to play in Mexico.

The Yankees were the only one of the three New York teams not to have lost a player to the Pasquels' raids. However, MacPhail was aware that the Mexican contingent was attempting to sign shortstop Phi Rizzuto to a reported three-year, $100,000 contract. George "Snuffy" Stirnweiss also had been an object of the Mexicans' interest. MacPhail, as in almost all of his baseball dealings, was the first of the club presidents to act in a passionate manner.

Claire Rutherford "Rud" Rennie, who was with *The New York Herald Tribune*, was the sportswriter referred to in the court order. Rennie, who had been seen in the Yankees' locker room, had been sent to Mexico by the newspaper a month earlier to view the operation of the then little-known Mexican League. His reports in *The Herald Tribune* had praised some aspects of the league and had criticized others. Rennie was quite surprised when he was named in the restraining order.

Daley rushed to Rennie's defense. He questioned MacPhail's quick and possibly inaccurate reaction to Rennie's presence in the locker room, a reaction that was not unexpected from the often impetuous and bombastic president of the Yankees. Arthur Daley wrote:

> The fiery redhead named Rennie in a lawsuit without ever asking him whether there was any truth to the charge. Then he withdrew the suit, which is akin to leaving Rud hung up between first and second without any umpires around to rule whether he is safe or out.[5]

Bernardo Pasquel reacted to MacPhail's legal action and promised that his organization would go to the United States Supreme Court in an attempt to offer better opportunities to players in the United States.

On May 5, the Dodgers sought and were granted a temporary restraining order that enjoined Jorge and Bernardo Pasquel from unlawfully interfering with the Dodgers by persuading their players to break their contracts. Owen and Olmo, who had been signed to Mexican League contracts, were listed in the injunction request. Pete Reiser, who was said to have turned down a three-year, $100,000 offer the preceding weekend, was also mentioned in the Dodgers' action. According to the Dodgers' petition, Mike Sandlock, Pee Wee Reese, Babe Herman, and Cookie Lavagetto were other Dodgers who had been mentioned as players whom the Mexican agents were interested in signing.

Five days later, Giants president Horace Stoneham announced that his club had also begun action against Jorge Pasquel and his brothers to prevent them from attempting to persuade members of his club to jump to the Mexican League. The Giants had already lost nine players to the Pasquels, which was the largest number of any of the teams in Organized Baseball.

The Giants were given a temporary restraining on May 11 by Justice William Hecht of the State Supreme Court.

The defense presented by the Pasquels in the Supreme Court was that Organized Baseball and its contracts were "monopolistic, unconscionable, illegal and against public policy."[6] The charge was leveled by Jerome Hess, who was the attorney for Jorge Pasquel and the Mexican League. Hess also was the attorney for the Mexican government in the United States.

President Horace Stoneham and the New York Giants went to court to seek an injunction against the raiding Pasquels (© S.F. Giants Archive).

Hess spoke to the issue of Organized Baseball's reserve clause in the standard player contract that gave a team sole and exclusive rights to a player's services for the duration of his professional baseball life. If the player is traded, that right passes to his new club. Hess argued, "The player cannot challenge any action by the club. His only recourse is to give up baseball as a career and as a source of livelihood."[7] He also

4 ♦ The Pasquels Move on Organized Baseball

noted the right of a club to terminate a player's contract on short notice. According to the defense, the Mexican League was offering players in the United States an opportunity to free themselves from bondage.

While the executives of the three New York teams were traveling "to and fro" to the courts in the city seeking injunctions against the Pasquels' Mexican League, Babe Ruth was making a trip to Mexico. His wife, daughter, and son-in-law flew out of La Guardia Field on May 15 for what they said was to be a 10-day to two-week vacation. Some were suggesting that he was going to Mexico to consider an offer from the Pasquels. Perhaps he would be named the manager of one of the teams or become the league's commissioner. Ruth had long wanted to manage in the major leagues after his playing days ended in 1935. He had lobbied hard to get the position with the Brooklyn Dodgers in the late 1930s, but MacPhail, the club president at the time, passed him over and named Leo Durocher to the post.

Bernardo was at the airport when the foursome departed, and Ruth was to be a guest of Jorge Pasquel during his stay in Mexico.

Before flying out of La Guardia, Ruth, claiming that baseball should be played all over the world, commented:

> I think the Pasquels are doing a fine thing for baseball and for their country. How far they will be able to go is hard to say, but they have a good start and in another year or two they really may have something big.[8]

Ruth's words would not endear himself to MacPhail, Rickey, Stoneham, and the other executives of Organized Baseball who were working to be done with the Pasquels.

The Ruth travel party arrived in Mexico City, and they were welcomed at the airport by Jorge, Mario, and 15,000 onlookers. That afternoon, Ruth was taken to the game between Vera Cruz and Tampico at Delta Park, and his foursome sat in Jorge's private box. The fans gave the "Babe" a warm Mexican welcome when he was "officially" introduced by Jorge Pasquel from the third-base line after the first inning.

Jorge Pasquel's Vera Cruz team was beaten by Tampico's Stevedores, 7–4, on the diamond. The diamond in Pasquel's ring far outclassed any of the jewelry worn by Ruth and his family.

Mexican Raiders in the Major Leagues

Ruth saw some familiar faces on the field during the game. Tampico manager Armando Marsans had been in the major leagues for eight seasons as an outfielder, including playing for the Yankees in 1917 and 1918 while Ruth was still with the Red Sox. Eight players who had followed the Pasquels' money south, including Gardella and Owen, were in the game. Bobby Estalella, who had come from the Athletics, hit a home run for the Blues.

Ruth's extended vacation included attending other ballgames, playing a few rounds of golf, attending a bullfight, and traveling. On May 17, during a round of golf, he told reporters that he had not signed any agreements with the Pasquels since his arrival and didn't plan to do so. It was also reported that the "Babe" was nine over par for nine holes during his outing at the Chapultepec Club.

When Ruth returned home on May 31, he was not the new commissioner of the Mexican League, but he applauded the Pasquels again for their efforts in their league. He appeared to be in agreement with the idea that a player should be free to make as much money as he could during his career, be it in the United States or elsewhere. However, there were also indications in what he had said during the trip that he was less than excited about the quality of baseball he saw being played in Mexico.

Soon after Ruth's departure from Mexico, Jorge Pasquel's interest turned to another ex–Yankee. He contacted long-time manager Joe McCarthy (1926–1946), who had recently resigned his post with New York, to talk about an unspecified position in the Mexican League. McCarthy did not take a position in the league, and, in 1948, he was named to manage the Boston Red Sox.

The Pasquels had been successful in bringing major leaguers from the United States to their league. Twenty-three players had made the jump in the hope of improving their financial situations and playing fulltime as "major leaguers" in another setting. The following is the list of players who had gone to Mexico along with the names of the clubs they had left to go south of the border

Ace Adams	New York Giants
Alex Carrasquel	Washington Senators

4 ♦ The Pasquels Move on Organized Baseball

Bobby Estalella	Philadelphia Athletics
Harry Feldman	New York Giants
Moe Franklin	Detroit Tigers [cut in spring training]
Danny Gardella	New York Giants
Roland Gladu	Brooklyn Dodgers
George Hausmann	New York Giants
Myron "Red" Hayworth	St. Louis Browns
Lou Klein	St. Louis Cardinals
Max Lanier	St. Louis Cardinals
Sal Maglie	New York Giants
Fred Martin	St. Louis Cardinals
Charlie Mead	New York Giants
Rene Monteagudo	Philadelphia Phillies
Luis Olmo	Brooklyn Dodgers
Roberto Ortiz	Washington Senators
Mickey Owen	Brooklyn Dodgers
Napoleon Reyes	New York Giants
James Steiner	Boston Red Sox
Vern Stephens	St. Louis Browns
Adrian Zabala	New York Giants
Roy Zimmerman	New York Giants

There were 10 major league teams that lost players to the Mexican League in 1946. The National League clubs had provided the most fertile soil for finding players to pick. The teams and the number of players the major league clubs lost were:

American League
Boston Red Sox [1]
Chicago White Sox [1]
Detroit Tigers [1]
Philadelphia Athletics [1]
St. Louis Browns [1]
Washington Senators [2]

National League
Brooklyn Dodgers [3]
New York Giants [9]
Philadelphia Phillies [1]
St. Louis Cardinals [3]

There were six teams that didn't lose any players to the Mexican League in 1946. Those teams were:

Mexican Raiders in the Major Leagues

American League
Cleveland Indians
New York Yankees

National League
Boston Braves
Chicago Cubs
Cincinnati Reds
Pittsburgh Pirates

♦ 5 ♦

Life as a Player in the Mexican League

The independent "outlaw" Mexican League, under the leadership of the Pasquels, proved to be too powerful for the rival Mexican National League. It was the Class B league's first season of affiliation with Organized Baseball. With the exception of the El Paso, Texas, club, all the teams in the league were located in Mexico. The teams began to experience financial difficulties early in the season. The clubs in Mexico City and Torreon soon dropped out of the league and their players were dispersed to other teams. On May 27, the Mexican National League, with its difficulties continuing to mount, was scuttled. The Pasquels had dispatched their opposition league in short order.

The Pasquels' league was working on ways to add additional players. They didn't want to be limited in the number of American imports they could place with the teams. On May 23, it was reported that the Mexican League had found a loophole whereby more American players could find places on the clubs' rosters. Earlier, the league had adopted a quota statement about foreign players that said that no more than nine foreign players could be on a team's roster and that no more than seven of those players could play at one time. The new agreement said that, for the time being, all Latin American players who had never played in Organized Baseball or in Cuban professional baseball would not be considered foreign players.

The Pasquels missed on adding two more players to their teams in early June. Pete Coscarart, an infielder with the Dodgers and the

Mexican Raiders in the Major Leagues

Pittsburgh Pirates from 1938 to 1945, was sold by the Pirates to San Diego of the Pacific Coast League. Initially, Coscarart said that he was making plans to play in Mexico rather than report to San Diego. He soon changed his tune and signed a contract to play in the Pacific Coast League. He said that he hoped that he would be able to climb back to the major leagues with a strong performance in San Diego.

The second player not to choose Mexico was a much more familiar name. On June 6, Alfonso Pasquel and Mickey Owen arrived in St. Louis with the avowed intention of signing Stan Musial, the Cardinals' 25-year-old outfielder, and having him return to Mexico with them. Musial had been discharged from military service in March, and the 1943 National League batting champion joined the Cardinals late for spring training. Pasquel's June visit was not the first time that his family had tried to lure Musial away from the Cards. They had contacted him earlier about leaving St. Louis.

Alfonso Pasquel and Owen visited Musial's hotel room and spread $65,000 in cashier's checks on his bed. Musial was told that this money was only a bonus for joining the Mexican League. There would be even more money available for him if he accepted the offer.

While Musial, who was making $13,500 with St. Louis, was considering the offer, Eddie Dyer, the Cards' manager, intervened, saying, "Stan, you've got two children. Do you want them to hear someone say, 'There are the kids of a guy who broke a contract'?"[1]

The Pasquels weren't any more successful this time with Musial than they had been in their other attempts. The Future Hall of Famer turned down the five-year contract, and he left Pasquel and Owen to talk with other members of the team about the benefits of playing south of the border.

Ernesto Carmona, president of the Mexico City club and one of the league's founders, saw a bright future in terms of attracting star players to the circuit. He was disappointed that the league had not yet been able to convince Bob Feller or Joe DiMaggio to jump to Mexico, but he was not giving up. He was hoping to have 10 or 12 additional major league stars in Mexico in 1947. That influx of players would be in conjunction with the opening of new ballparks in the league.

The courts in the United States continued to play a role in the

5 ♦ Life as a Player in the Mexican League

"raider situation." The Dodgers were dealt a blow in a St. Louis court in early June when they lost their request for a permanent injunction against the Mexican League. Federal Judge Rubey M. Hulen dismissed the action against Jorge and Bernardo Pasquel, two agents, and a local sportswriter who had been named in the earlier temporary injunction. Hulen dismissed the suit because of lack of evidence and because four of the five were non-residents of the eastern Missouri district.

The Yankees and the Giants had their requests for permanent injunctions delayed until October, but they still would have the power of temporary injunctions behind them.

Even though Larry MacPhail, Horace Stoneham, and Branch Rickey had some success in the courts, most owners were not happy with their attempts to handle the Pasquels and the Mexican League in that manner. They were willing to give the Mexican League time to disappear through financial attrition. They were fearful that an approach to their problem through the courts might also lead to consideration of the legality of a player's contract and the reserve clause. That could prove to be the owners' greatest nightmare.

A ruling on May 5, 1946, had alerted Organized Baseball to the role that the courts could play in disputes between a player and his team. In an unprecedented decision, Assistant United States Attorney Tom A. Durham ruled that the Seattle Rainiers of the Pacific Coast League must reinstate infielder Al Niemec, who had played for them before entering military service. The Rainiers had released Niemec, and he appealed to the Selective Service Board for reinstatement to his former job. Referring to the GI Bill of Rights, Durham ruled:

> Baseball is no different than a store or a machine shop.... The law is simple. A veteran rates his job back and we intend to see that the law is carried out. We are not interested in whether or not Niemec plays with the Rainiers, but they will have to carry him on the club and pay him his salary.[2]

With an increased sensitivity to the role the courts might play in player disputes, some of the owners were jittery:

> in doing so [going to the courts], the clubs had invited legal attention to the potentially explosive issue of the Uniform

Player's Contract with its reserve clause and ten-day severance provision. In the hearing for the injunction sought by the Yankees the Pasquels' attorney argued that Organized Baseball constituted an illegal monopoly, but he also raised the issue of the player's contract and Court Justice Julius Miller eventually granted the injunction the Yankees sought, and he chastised the Pasquels for seducing employees to break contracts they'd voluntarily entered into. But before he made his decision, Miller asked what were to prove troubling questions about the contract and whether in its present form it was absolutely essential to the continued health of the game.[3]

Frederick Turner, in the book *When The Boys Came Back: Baseball and 1946*, wrote:

The lawyers for the Yankees, Dodgers, and Giants had been speaking truthfully in their pleas before the court when they argued that baseball, "as we know it," was founded on the standard contract with its reserve clause. If a club's exclusive rights to a player's services were ever to be successfully challenged, its signings, its farm systems, and its player transactions would topple, leaving the chaos of free agency and an open market.[4]

Sam Breadon, the president of the Cardinals, made a trip to Mexico to meet with Jorge Pasquel in mid–June. Breadon, who was also vice president of the National League, said that he was taking the trip on his own, and that he was not on "official" league business. Breadon had not been exempted from the Pasquels' moves. The Cardinals had lost three players to the Mexican League — pitchers Max Lanier and Fred Martin and infielder Lou Klein. The Pasquels also had attempted to sign Musial and other Cards.

The initial thought was that Breadon was on a peace mission, trying to find a way to end the war between Organized Baseball and the Pasquels. There was also an interesting but quite unlikely suggestion that Breadon was trying to sell the Cardinals to the Pasquels, but the Cards' president quickly put that idea to rest.

When Chandler heard about Breadon's trip to Mexico, which went against his order that owners not have individual contact with Jorge Pasquel, the commissioner was quite displeased. Initially, he threatened Breadon with a large fine and a suspension.

5 ♦ Life as a Player in the Mexican League

Breadon was seen by some as the epitome of what players in the United States were having to deal with. An article in *Newsweek* written by John Lardner, assessed the Mexican situation and described Breadon's approach to those players who were under his control and wondered why more of them had not left for Mexico:

> Mr. Samuel Breadon's idea of a living wage is considerably narrower than Senor Jorge Pasquel's. However, Mr. Breadon offers his boys a World Series by way of (a) bonus.... If some of them waver in the near future, Samuel can spare the talent.[5]

Following his initial conversations with Jorge Pasquel, Breadon attended a game as the guest of Bernardo and Mario Pasquel. He watched Martin, a former Cardinal, pitch for Mexico City and drop a 3–1 decision to Nuevo Laredo. Agapito Mayor, who was on his way to a 20–9 campaign, was the winning pitcher. Mayor had pitched in the early 1940s for Springfield, Massachusetts, of the Eastern League.

Sam Breadon, the president of the St. Louis Cardinals, made a trip to Mexico in June 1946 and met with Jorge Pasquel. Breadon's visit did not please commissioner A.B. Chandler (National Baseball Hall of Fame Library, Cooperstown, N.Y.).

Upon Breadon's return from Mexico on June 22, he was summoned by Chandler to report to his Cincinnati, Ohio, office to meet with him and National League president Ford Frick. Chandler wanted to hear about his conversations with the Pasquels. When Breadon failed to attend the meeting scheduled for the Monday following his return, he was given a day of grace by Chandler. However, after he failed to appear on Tuesday, Chandler informed him by letter that he had been fined $5,000. Breadon's immediate defense was that he had told Jorge Pasquel that he was making the trip to Mexico on his own and to report about it to the commissioner would make it appear as if he was not being truthful. Chandler eventually rescinded the fine.

Near the end of July, there was a report that Breadon and the Pasquels had come to an agreement that the baseball interests in both countries would recognize each other and work together. Breadon denied knowing anything about the "peace plan," and it was quickly brushed off by others in official capacities in Organized Baseball.

Breadon did say that he believed that the Pasquels were in baseball to stay, and that their challenge was to be a serious one. They were well-connected politically and they appeared to have significant amounts of money behind their baseball venture.

When the owners met for their regularly scheduled gathering the day before the All-Star Game in July, there wasn't any mention of either of the two issues that had buzzed around Organized Baseball that season. The meeting proceeded as if the American Baseball Guild (A.B.G.) and the Mexican League didn't exist.

However, John Drebinger, writing in the *New York Times*, painted a clear picture about the players' situations.

> The very fact that for years the owners brazenly took to themselves the right to make all the rules governing options, contract dispensations, sales and minor league classifications without ever consulting the players in the formulation of these rules is in itself an astonishing piece of effrontery....[6]

Drebinger saw the gullibility of young kids who were willing to sign anything and do anything for a chance to play in the major leagues as the key that handed control to ownership. In 1946, as in a few periods in the past, some players were seeing things in a different manner and were beginning to question the way things were.

While the ballplayers in the states were making some potential long-term improvements in their playing conditions, those who had gone to Mexico were experiencing disappointments. Stephens had found the conditions that greeted him in Mexico to be unacceptable, and he headed back to the Browns after a few days in his new situa-

5 ♦ Life as a Player in the Mexican League

tion. He came back before Organized Baseball's Opening Day, and he was not subject to the 5-year suspension that Chandler had handed down. Owen lasted until August before he packed his bags with the hope of returning to baseball with the Dodgers.

Most of the 23 players who had taken the Pasquels' money were making much more than they would have made in the states, but, for most of them, it proved not to be worth the difficulties they found.

Mexico City is a little over 8,000 feet above sea level, and the rarified air often made it difficult for players to catch their breath. No stadium in the majors at the time approached the atmospheric conditions offered in the Mexican League. In a game early in the season, there was a five-minute delay while a player caught his breath after hitting a triple. Former Cincinnati pitcher Tommy De La Cruz, who had been in Mexico since 1945, was recovering from surgery on his leg, but was having difficulty getting himself into condition after the injury was healed. Because of the altitude, De La Cruz could not do as much running as was necessary to get himself in shape to pitch.

Pitchers suffered and hitters gained from the high altitude. Long fly balls sometimes turned into 500-foot home runs. Danny Gardella and Roberto Ortiz, former Washington Senator outfielder, had each launched lengthy, tape-measure blasts.

A number of the players were suffering from gastro-intestinal problems that had resulted from the change of diet they encountered in Mexico. In May, it was announced that the Pasquels planned to have special chefs for the players so that they would have "familiar" food available for them.

The three-games-a-week schedule provided a lot of free time—often too much. Players from the states, who were used to playing at least six days each week during the season, had difficulty finding things to do in their spare time, especially in a foreign country where they didn't understand the language. When the schedule was expanded to four games per week, that problem was lessened a bit.

The ballparks were far below the quality of those in the United States, and that was especially problematic for the players. Delta Park, with advertisements for liquor and soft drinks displayed on the outfield walls, was closest to the playing fields in Organized Baseball, but even it was not as good as those in the states. The word "sandlot" would be an apt description for the other Mexican League fields. There wasn't any grass in the infields, and the ground was hard and rocky, which especially was not welcomed by infielders. Difficult and unexpected bounces were regular occurrences for them. It wasn't a series of "smooth rolls" in the outfields either. Rickety wooden stands provided the seating facilities in many of the parks.

Playing the outfield in Tampico could become a very strange adventure. The bleachers extended to the foul pole. A set of railroad tracks ran through the outfield, inside the outfield fence. An outfielder had to be cautious when backing up to catch a fly ball, lest he trip on the rails of steel. Play was suspended for a time on some afternoons when the gates in right and left fields were opened so that a train could pass through the ballpark.

The dugouts in the ballparks were small and poorly ventilated, and they soon became offensive in terms of odor. Some players never ventured into the dugout, but sat or laid outside them on the dirt or grass. Many of the parks didn't have locker rooms and showers, so the players had to dress and shower in their hotel rooms.

In May, Jorge Pasquel conferred with New York architect John Sloan about constructing new modern parks throughout the league. The Pasquels were promising a new $2,000,000 baseball stadium in Mexico City, with a seating capacity of 45,000, for the 1947 season. Sloan had been the designer of the Hipodromo de las Americas and other race tracks. The Pasquels also were planning to have new ballparks built for every team in the league in the near future. All of this was being generated by the excitement spawned by the arrival of the stars from the States.

The 1946 season was an especially rainy one, and that didn't help the conditions for the ballplayers. At times the electricity would go out during a storm and the game had to be stopped.

Puebla, an ancient town, was generally ranked as the least desirable among the cities and towns in the league. The hotel accommodations were horrible, and, when a team had to be there for an extended period of time, there was nothing to do but suffer through the terrible conditions.

5 ♦ Life as a Player in the Mexican League

Travel to some places in the league was both arduous and dangerous, especially when the buses were attempting to navigate over the winding mountains. Owen commented about air travel, which was sometimes an alternative to the bus. The ex-Dodger catcher, who had benefited in Brooklyn where MacPhail who had been the first to institute air travel in the majors, had known the benefits and relative comfort of that form of transportation. Owen described landing fields in Mexico that were no more than pastures and said, "Coming in for a landing we'd look out and see eight or 10 of those big black Mexican vultures waiting for us. That's one of the things I remember best about Mexico — those vultures."[7]

Jorge Pasquel was hoping to remedy the travel difficulties for the players by extending the amount of airplane travel for the clubs. He was toying with the idea of purchasing a large transport plane for moving teams from one city to another. He also considered the possibility of using the plane himself for lion hunts in Africa during the off-season.

Those who had left Organized Baseball for promises of riches south of the border had pocketed more money but also had suffered through endless rain, long and uncomfortable bus rides, strange food, and inferior lighting in substandard ballparks.

As the season progressed, some of the non–U.S. players in the league began to express anger and resentment about the large salaries being paid to the players that the Pasquels had recruited. Most of the new additions hadn't become the stars of their clubs, and the high salaries didn't seem to be justified in the opinions of the other players.

Owen left the Vera Cruz club at the end of July and headed home, hoping to resume his career with the Dodgers. On August 9, Dodger outfielder Augie Galan reported that star players on the major league clubs had been flooded with a new barrage of letters from Jorge Pasquel, who was angry about Owen's defection. Pasquel had proclaimed war again on the major leagues. He was attempting to line up other players to replace those like Owen and Vern Stephens who had broken their contracts and commitments to him. Ted Williams and Johnny Pesky of the Red Sox were two of the many players that Pasquel was soliciting. The president of the Mexican League said that he would give

Williams a signed, blank check, and that he could fill in the amount of his salary.

Jorge Pasquel was also angry and disappointed by the way the season had unfolded for the pair of clubs that he and his brothers owned. The Mexico City Reds did play well through much of the campaign, but they failed to overtake Tampico for the league's ultimate crown — the pennant. Most of Pasquel's disappointment was aimed at the Vera Cruz Blues. The club had the largest group of players who had come from Organized Baseball. The Blues struggled on the field and in the relationships between the players, and they hung around the bottom of the loop for most of the season. Vera Cruz, with the league's largest payroll, finished in seventh place, beating out only the San Luis Potosi Tuneros.

In late August, the Mexican League signed another player, but Jorge Pasquel, in a goodwill gesture toward Organized Baseball, ordered that the contract be withdrawn. The Nuevo Laredo team inked 26-year-old outfielder Hooper Triplett, who had been permanently banned from professional baseball in the United States for having bet on his own team. At the time of the wager, Triplett was hitting .314 for the Columbus, Georgia, Cardinals of the Sally League. Following the withdrawal of the contract to Triplett, the diplomatic Pasquel said his league would not sign an American player who had been expelled for betting against his own club.

The league began to struggle as the season passed. There was a fall-off in terms of fan interest in some places, a few defections by imports, and financial difficulties. After the initial swelling of fan support, the ballparks began to display a growing number of empty seats. An especially rainy summer also didn't help the attendance figures. It all ended when the 1946 postseason was cancelled.

The 23 players who had come to Mexico played for several clubs. Jorge Pasquel had assigned the largest group to Vera Cruz. Monterrey was the only club without an import from the United States. Almost all of those that left Organized Baseball came from one of three categories. Some were American and had not previously played baseball outside the United States. Another group had played during the winter months in Latin America. The third and final group consisted of

5 ♦ Life as a Player in the Mexican League

Latin Americans who had played in their own countries and had reached the major leagues in the United States.

The following is a list of the 23 players and the teams they were with in 1946:

Ace Adams	Vera Cruz
Alex Carrasquel	Vera Cruz, Mexico City
Bobby Estalella	Vera Cruz, San Luis Potosi
Harry Feldman	Vera Cruz
Moe Franklin	Tampico
Danny Gardella	Vera Cruz
Roland Gladu	Nuevo Laredo
George Hausmann	Torreon
Myron "Red" Hayworth	Torreon
Lou Klein	Vera Cruz
Max Lanier	Vera Cruz
Sal Maglie	Puebla
Fred Martin	Mexico City
Charlie Mead	Vera Cruz
Rene Monteagudo	Torreon
Luis Olmo	Mexico City, Vera Cruz
Roberto Ortiz	Mexico City
Mickey Owen	Vera Cruz
Napoleon Reyes	Puebla
Jim Steiner	Nuevo Laredo
Vern Stephens	Vera Cruz
Adrian Zabala	Puebla
Roy Zimmerman	Nuevo Laredo

The following is a list of the number of players who were with the teams in the Mexican League either full or part time in 1946:

Mexico City	4
Nuevo Laredo	3
Puebla	3
San Luis Potosi	1

Mexican Raiders in the Major Leagues

Tampico	1
Torreon	3
Vera Cruz	11

In the following chapters I will add material about the professional background of each of the players and will also add information about some aspects of his time playing in the Mexican League. Through these accounts, more will be learned about the players, the Pasquels, the Mexican League, the 1946 season, and beyond the initial "Mexican raid."

Chandler might have had a vision of a new day as he watched the 1946 season unfold. When he was elected in 1945, he was chosen mainly because the owners thought that they could control him more easily than they had been able to handle Landis. The American Baseball Guild had challenged Chandler and the owners to pay more attention to the wishes of the players. The struggle with the Mexican League added more pressure on the commissioner and management. In August, Chandler addressed the owners and tried to awaken them to the financial realities of the times. Regarding the invasion of Jorge Pasquel and his brothers, he challenged the owners to do a better job providing for the players. He added:

> You can't blame kids for grabbing the big money he's putting out, but he can't keep that up, and won't.[8]

♦ 6 ♦

Danny Gardella: The Pasquels' First Catch

On February 19, 1946, Danny Gardella, an outfielder with the New York Giants, announced that he was jumping to the "outlaw" Mexican League. He was the first major league player to take an offer from Jorge Pasquel and head to Mexico to play baseball there. Twenty-two others followed this very average ballplayer who saw an opportunity to better himself financially and, perhaps, become a star, and he leapt at it.

Gardella made his major league debut on May 14, 1944, at age 24. He had been a shipyard worker earlier in 1944, loading supply ships on the docks in Jersey City, New Jersey, when he was "discovered" while playing semi-pro ball with a shipyard team. He was signed by the Giants, and he played for six weeks with the club's minor league team in Jersey City.

After arriving at the Polo Grounds, the 5'7½", 160-pound, left-handed hitting and throwing outfielder from the Bronx hit .250 in 47 games with the fifth-place Giants. He played in 121 games the following season, hitting .272 with 18 home runs and 71 RBI. That year his brother Al, a left-handed hitting first baseman, also played with the club, appearing in 16 games.

Gardella was a good "fill-in player" for a wartime club, but with all of the players returning from World War II, he probably was not going be an important cog for the Giants during the 1946 season. He was one of the wartime players who possibly would be lost in the shuffle and sent to the minors for the campaign. No doubt Gardella was aware of his plight.

Mexican Raiders in the Major Leagues

He was described in this manner:

> He was an undisciplined hitter with big holes in his swing, and he had severe defensive liabilities. He could hit for distance, though, and manager Mel Ott had to go along with him because he had no one better (in 1944 and 1945). At bat, Gardella said he could overcome some of his deficiencies because he was very strong despite his small stature. Gardella was one of the first players to regularly lift weights and in the Polo Grounds where the Giants played he could muscle the ball down its short foul lines for home runs.[1]

The Giants' outfielder was also a genuine eccentric, and that quality didn't endear him to the club's management. He would grace the clubhouse or the trains on which the team traveled with operatic outbursts, and he was labeled "a crooner" all along his baseball journeys. He said, "I loved music, particularly operatic music, and I would uninhibitedly burst out in song from time to time. What the hell, why not sing and holler? You're young, you're healthy, and you're playing baseball. You're also nitwit enough not to remember anybody else's misery. So, I sang."[2]

Gardella exhibited his eccentricity in another event. On May 24, 1945, he left a suicide note for his roommate and teammate Napoleon Reyes in their hotel room during a trip to play the Reds in Cincinnati. When Reyes returned to the room a few minutes later, he came across the note and noticed an open window. He rushed to the window and discovered Danny hanging from the window ledge several stories above the street. Gardella had a broad grim on his face as if to say, "I got you!"

Gardella had met Jorge Pasquel in January 1946, at Al Roon's midtown Manhattan gym where he worked during the off-season. The job helped him pay his bills and let him keep in shape. Both Gardella and Pasquel were physical fitness junkies, and the power generated from Gardella's small frame attested to his strength. Pasquel, the charismatic and aggressive businessman, was drawn to Gardella, the eccentric and fun-loving major leaguer. Gardella supervised Pasquel's workouts, and Danny's gift of gab and occasional song for the customers opened communication between the two men.

Pasquel told Gardella about his plans to bring ballplayers from the United States to play in the Mexican League, and his hopes to develop his league so that it would become the same quality as the major leagues in the states. He described his grand plan to develop his league so that it would eventually be capable of competing with the American and National Leagues. Pasquel sowed a seed in Gardella's mind when he told him that he needed players in Mexico and to give him a call if he were ever interested.

Gardella's contract for 1945 was $4,500, and when the Giants sent him a contract for only an additional $500 for 1946, he sent it back to the club unsigned. The Giants couldn't care less about Gardella's response to the contract, and he was snubbed after he returned it without a signature. He later claimed that the team retaliated by giving him the wrong information about when the train to spring training in Miami was scheduled to leave New York, and he missed being on it. The Giants' position was that his raise was $500, and that was the end of it.

Eddie Brannick, the club's traveling secretary and the front man for owner Horace Stoneham, was not a person with whom one tangled. Players were there to play under the conditions set by management, and were not to make waves. That was the way the business of the of the game was to be, and Gardella discovered quickly that Brannick accepted nothing other than that approach.

The Giants' outfielder had had his moments with Brannick in the past. Once, during a night train trip to Chicago, Gardella climbed into the luggage rack above his train seat and tied himself to it with his belt. When Brannick came through the car for a check of the players, Gardella swung down and dangled in front of the "inspector." Brannick was enraged by Gardella's antics. It was not the way to befriend someone who already didn't care for you.

Gardella's troubles with the Giants in 1946 began with the unsigned contract and continued when he missed the train from New York to Miami. Upon arrival at the Giants' training site, the tardy outfielder was informed by manager Mel Ott, who had played for the club since 1926 and had been its playing manager since 1942, that he would not be allowed to stay in the team's hotel or participate in workouts until he put his signature on the contract. Ott did relent and allowed Gardella to take the field with other players and have a night's stay at one of the "overflow" facilities that the Giants were using to house the large number of players who were in the camp. However, Ott informed him that both "privileges" would end the following day if the contract was not signed.

When Gardella arrived at the dining room of the upscale Venetian Hotel, the largest hotel in the city and the facility that housed the most important Giant players, he was stopped by Brannick, who said that his sleeveless sweater was not suitable attire. The two men engaged in a loud confrontation, and by the time Gardella was finished, he had banged one more nail into his Giant coffin. An angry Ott, upon hearing about the dining room face-off, informed trainer Willie Schaeffer that even if Gardella signed his contract the following day he was still not to get a uniform and engage in team workouts. Ott said, "This fellow apparently has to be taught that players of his type are no longer of great importance in the major leagues, now that the war is over."[3]

At that point, Gardella was leaning toward signing the contract. However, Brannick and Ott had both had their fill of the outfielder. Ott told Gardella that even if he signed the disputed contract he was finished with the Giants, and they had put him on the auction block and that he would go to the highest bidder. Ott made his point when he told the recalcitrant outfielder that several minor league clubs had expressed interest in acquiring his services.

Gardella disappeared from the Giants' training facility, and he

Danny Gardella's difficult spring training with the New York Giants hastened his decision to take Jorge Pasquel's offer and head to Mexico (National Baseball Hall of Fame Library, Cooperstown, N.Y.).

reappeared four days later to announce that he had signed a contract to play in Mexico. Gardella had remembered Jorge Pasquel's invitation to come to his country, and he had acted on it.

Gardella was accompanied at the time of the announcement by Robert Janis, who he described as his personal agent and as an agent for Jorge Pasquel. Gardella said that he had signed a five-year contract to play in Mexico. His salary for the first year would be $8,000 to go along with a $5,000 signing bonus. That amount of money was more than twice what he would have received for a season with the Giants.

He also had been advised that he would save money because of the lower taxes in Mexico. However, in early April, the Internal Revenue Service announced that American citizens who went to Mexico to play baseball would be required to pay taxes in the United States. The amount paid in Mexico would be deducted from the amount they owed to the IRS on their Mexican wages.

Janis said that three other major leaguers had been signed to play south of the border. They were the Giants' Reyes and Adrian Zabala and the Brooklyn Dodgers' Luis Olmo.

Jorge Pasquel sent a private plane to Miami to take Gardella to Mexico City. The new Mexican Leaguer left Kate, his girlfriend of two years, behind in New York City, but she had been very supportive of his new venture. Kate was in college at the time, studying to become a teacher. When the plane arrived in Mexico City, it was greeted by the five Pasquel brothers and Manuel Avila Camacho, the president of Mexico. Gardella felt quite important indeed.

Upon arriving, Gardella said, "I'm mighty glad I'm no longer connected with the New York Giants.... They are paying me more here, so why shouldn't I play in Mexico?"[4]

When he hit the playing field for the Vera Cruz Blues, one of the two teams owned by the Pasquels, manager Ramon Bragana tried him in outfield positions other than his familiar left field, and also at first base, where he had played in only 15 games with the Giants in 1945. Playing first base went contrary to his previous experience. Players who were at that position were usually much taller than he was. On the other hand, Gardella had never been known as anything more than a decent outfielder, and some would not even have given him that much credit. First base became his primary position with his new team.

The season's opening game on March 21 featured the Pasquels' two teams, Vera Cruz and the Mexico City Reds, matching up in front of a large and raucous crowd at Delta Park. The Blues won the opener, 12–5, with Gardella slugging a two-run homer in leading his club to the victory. Two other former major leaguers from the United States, Alejandro Carrasquel and Roberto Estalella, did not see action for Vera Cruz. The Reds' Olmo, the former Dodger, homered for the losers.

The Pasquels were hoping to find additional players who would like to join their clubs in Mexico. Janis predicted that there would be serious problems in the ranks of the Giants and the Dodgers if the two clubs didn't move away from their harsh treatment of their players, and they would provide a fertile field out of which the Pasquels could harvest more players.

The Giants' Brannick responded to Janis' prediction and downplayed Gardella's signing, saying, "If Janis thinks that there is discontent among the Giants he is far off the beam. I know Mr. Stoneham did not regret the jumping of Danny Gardella to the Mexican League. What the Mexican said sounds ridiculous to me."[5]

Offensively, Gardella had hits in his first seven games before he went 0-for-4 in the next contest. He was productive during the first half of the season, hitting above the .300 mark and delivering key hits in the clutch for the Blues. However, the team that had been stocked with players brought in from the major leagues was not playing up to Gardella's expectations of those of the Pasquels. The players were not blending together as a team, and the club was struggling in the bottom half of the league's standings.

On April 20, Gardella hit two homers, but in a 4–3 losing effort against the Monterrey Sultans. Charley Mead, another former Giant who was making his Mexican League debut in right field, and catcher Mickey Owen both went hitless for Vera Cruz.

On June 2, Vera Cruz was in seventh place with a 13–20 mark. San Luis Potosi was a game behind them in the league's basement. Monterrey had a 23–10 record and was sitting at the top of the league, holding a three-game advantage over the Tampico Cotton Pickers. The top three teams in the leagues—Monterrey, Tampico, and Mexico City—were made up mainly of black players and others from Latin American countries. The weaker teams, like the Blues, consisted mainly of white players from the United States and other places.

Gardella was chosen for the Southern squad for the Mexican League All-Star Game. His team had representation from the Mexico City, Puebla, San Luis Potosi, and Vera Cruz clubs. The Northern team had players from Monterrey, Nuevo Laredo, Tampico, and Torreon.

The game was played on July 9, the same day that the major leaguers in the states were holding their Mid-Summer Classic at Fenway Park, Boston. It also was the day following the presidential election in Mexico, and new president Miguel Aleman was at Jorge Pasquel's side during the game. Pasquel had been a major financial supporter of the newly elected president.

The Americans throttled the Nationals, 12–0, in Boston, and the South topped the North, 11–8, in Mexico City.

United States Admiral William F. Halsey, a "good will" guest in Mexico, threw out the ceremonial first pitch. United States Ambassador Walter Thurston also was in attendance for the game that matched the best in Mexican League baseball in 1946.

Gardella put on another show, powering two more home runs as 12,000 fans watched the All-Stars.

The league's statistics on August 1 showed that the ex-Giant was tied for third place in the home-run race with 10 round-trippers. Ex–Washington Senators player Roberto Ortiz was leading the loop with 16 homers.

However, as the season progressed, Gardella became bored by having too many days off, and by being in a foreign country where he was not fluent in the native language. He longed to have Kate with him, and he finally proposed to her. Soon, she joined him in Mexico, and they were married.

The season ceased to be enjoyable for Gardella. Baseball had always been fun for the New York native, but the game had become an exercise in drudgery in Mexico.

Vera Cruz, Gardella's club, continued to struggle and ended up not being the success that the Pasquels hoped that it would be. They had "bought" the team with their money, and they were quite angry when the club sputtered through the season. It was as if all the money they had invested in making the Blues the potential league champion had gone down the drain. The irony was that Tampico, which had only one American import (Moe Franklin), raced to the pennant and raised the championship flag. They were a "team" and not a group of "hired guns" in search of a pennant. Tampico did all the little things involving pitching, hitting and base running that led to victories.

Gardella's Blues' final game of the season was against Puebla. Although he had lost interest in the campaign by that time and returning to the United States was but a day away, the matchup would determine whether Vera Cruz or the San Luis Potosi club finished in the league's basement. A victory by Vera Cruz would give them the seventh spot in the final standings and save them from utter disappointment and embarrassment.

Even though it was a rainy day in Mexico City, Delta Park was filled to capacity. The sun made its appearance as the game began, but the soggy conditions on the field greeted the players as they went to their positions. Managers Bragana and Aldolfo Luque had their rosters made out for the game. Gardella was at first base for Vera Cruz and the rest of the infield had Chile Gomez at second, Lou Klein at shortstop, and Buster Clarkson at third base.

Bernardo Pasquel was in the family box with president Aleman, but Jorge was not in attendance for the finale.

Max Lanier, who had begun the season with the St. Louis Cardinals, was on the mound for the Blues, and they were down, 4–0, after Puebla's first at-bat. Zabala, a former teammate of Gardella with the Giants, was Luque's choice to go to the hill. He didn't fare any better than Lanier as he also gave up four runs to tie the game, 4–4. Gardella struck out in the middle of the rally.

In the sixth inning, Gardella's home run over the center-field fence off Zabala was part of a seven-run rally to make the score 11–4 in favor of the Blues.

Both managers went to the mound during the game to pitch. Bragana had pitched in the Mexican League since 1938, and he was 9–16 in 1946. He held the lead in relief for the victorious Blues. In the Blues' final at-bat, Luque was on the hill for Puebla. Unlike Bragana, the 56-year-old Luque had not pitched in a game for 11 years until his appearance on the final day of the season. He had finished his 20-year National League career in 1935 as a pitcher for the Giants. Luque had made relief appearances in two games for the Cincinnati Reds against the Chicago White Sox in the ill-fated 1919 World Series. In 1946, Luque pitched one scoreless inning, mixing slow with slower. He recorded one strikeout, and Gardella was the player to go down swinging.

The Blues were spared the disgrace of ending the season in last place. However, their seventh-place finish was still difficult for Gardella, other players, and the Pasquels to accept.

That would be the end of Gardella's Mexican League experience. He would never receive the $500 prize he had won on the final day of the season when his home run went into the mouth of the smiling man on the Chiclets billboard. The year of the sizeable salaries was over. Near the end of the season, the Pasquels began to inform players that their salaries would be cut for the 1947 season. Gardella's contract would put him back to the amount he had made with the Giants before his Mexican sojourn.

A few hours after the game, Gardella and his wife were on an airplane heading for New York City. When the plane touched down, they were home. Their Mexican adventure was finished. Behind Gardella was a season of expectation that had turned to disappointment. The Mexican League had failed to put a scare into the minds and wallets of major league owners. Gardella's season had begun well. He hit the ball and was one of the club's offensive leaders. However, he was mired in a slump during much of the later part of the summer. He carried his record for the 1946 season with him. It read:

> Batting average: .275, Games: 100, At-bats: 378, Runs: 56, Hits: 104, Total Bases: 174, Doubles: 23, Triples: 4, Home Runs: 13, RBI: 64, Bases on Balls: 60, Strikeouts: 34, Stolen Bases: 5, Slugging Percentage: .460.[6]

♦ 7 ♦

Vernon Stephens: A Very Short Sojourn South

When the St. Louis Browns' Vernon "Junior" Stephens signed a contract to play baseball in the Mexican League, the Pasquels had acquired a gem from Organized Baseball in the United States. Stephens was an outstanding acquisition. He was not a "has-been" or a "second-string holdout" who was in spring training fighting for a spot along with many of the game's top players who were returning after World War II. The Browns would suffer the loss of the talented Stephens more than most of the other teams that the Pasquels had set their eyes on raiding, because they had a much smaller pool of quality players.

Stephens, who was born on October 23, 1920, in McAlister, New Mexico, signed with the Browns for a $500 bonus in 1938 at age 17. He played two games for Springfield, Illinois, of the Three-I League, and then was sent by the Browns to Johnstown, Pennsylvania, of the Middle Atlantic League, where he hit .257. The following year, while playing for Mayfield, Kentucky, of the Class-D Kitty League, Stephens led the circuit in batting with a .361 average, in RBI with 123, and in doubles with 44.

In 1940, he was with San Antonio of the Texas League and led that circuit with 97 RBI. In 1941, Stephens spent most of the campaign with Triple-A Toledo of the American Association. He joined the Browns late in the season and made his major league debut September 13, playing three games after his call-up.

Stephens arrived fulltime in the majors in 1942, playing shortstop for the Browns in 145 games. He hit .294 with 14 home runs and 92

RBI. He was on the All-Star team the following season, and he hit .289 while banging 22 homers and driving in 91 runs.

The 1944 campaign was special for Stephens and the Browns, who finished one game ahead of Detroit in the American League. It was the Browns' only pennant in St. Louis. They went on to meet the St. Louis Cardinals in the World Series, losing 4 games to 2. Stephens struggled to a .227 average in the series after being at or near the top of a number of offensive categories during the regular season. He led the league with 109 RBI, finished second in homers with 20, and was on the All-Star team again. Stephens was third in the voting for the league's Most Valuable Player Award behind Detroit Tigers pitchers Hal Newhouser and Dizzy Trout.

In 1945, the Browns slipped to third place behind Detroit and Washington in what was to be the final season of wartime baseball. The St. Louis shortstop had another quality season, leading the league with 24 home runs and posting a league-best .961 fielding percentage for all players at his position.

The Browns, along with the Chicago Cubs, the Chicago White Sox, and the Pittsburgh Pirates, held their spring training camps in California. Browns vice president Bill DeWitt traveled to Anaheim, California, in late February when it appeared as if Stephens was going to be a holdout, which would be a serious matter for the club. The team had offered the American League home run champion $13,000 for the 1946 season, and he had asked for $17,500.

After weeks of haggling over a new contract, Stephens spoke about being a holdout for 1946. He soon was contacted by Jorge Pasquel. The Pasquels were working the spring training sites in Florida, where the majority of the major league clubs had their spring training facilities. He made it to California, and he and Stephens sat down and talked. The result of the conversations was a Mexican League contract for the shortstop. On March 30, he agreed to a five-year contract with an annual salary of not less than the $17,500 he had asked for from the Browns. He would be heading to play for the Vera Cruz Blues, where he would become a teammate of Danny Gardella and others who had defected from the United States

After the signing was announced, Richard Muckerman, the president of the Browns, appeared to be taking a casual stance with regard to the Mexican League and a hands-off attitude about the club's former shortstop. He commented about the Mexican League and its recent success in attracting players to go south of the border, saying, "We're not concerned."[1] When the conversation turned to Stephens, Muckerman added, "We've made our proposition to Stephens and are waiting for him to report. We haven't heard from him yet."[2]

Browns' manager Luke Sewell played down the loss of Stephens and intimated that he believed that the Mexican League was not getting the quality player that it believed it had signed. He continued to cover his bases, saying that he hadn't been counting on the 25 year old to be the club's shortstop in 1946. He added that he was planning to use Mark Christman, who was a better fielder than Stephens."

Stephens took a midnight flight from California to Nuevo Laredo on a plane chartered by Jorge Pasquel. He spent the night at Alfonso Pasquel's home there and then made the second lap of the journey to Mexico City. Before leaving Nuevo Laredo, Stephens announced, "I won't have anything to do with the Browns unless they call me."[3]

He had his first exposure to Mexican League baseball when he attended a game at Delta Park on March 30 and watched as Vera Cruz defeated Nuevo Laredo. At one point in the game, Stephens was introduced to the crowd, and he received a huge reception from the fans.

As it turned out, some would be happy to see him at shortstop and others would not be. Upon Stephens' arrival, Jorge Pasquel dispensed the team's former sure-handed shortstop, Frank Rizutti, to the Mexico City Reds. Rizutti had played for the New York Giants in 1939 under the name of Frank Scalzi, and had been in the Mexican League in 1940, becoming a fan favorite with the Blues. His move to Mexico City was neither a sale nor a trade. Pasquel had simply sent him there. Stephens would not give the club the defense that Rizutti was expected to provide, but Pasquel believed that he would be much more of an offensive threat.

After the game, Stephens and Jorge Pasquel talked for nearly three hours in Pasaquel's office, then the two men headed for Pasquel's Mexico City home, where they spent the night. It was a five-story "palace" that included a gymnasium, a massive closet that contained his overwhelming clothing collection, and a seven-car garage.

The next day, March 31, Stephens was at shortstop in the Blues' lineup as Vera Cruz battled Nuevo Laredo again. His single in the bottom of the ninth inning drove in the winning run in the Blues' 5–4 victory. He played flawlessly in the field and started a pair of double plays.

Two fellow transplants to the Blues also aided in the victory. Gardella singled in the bottom of the ninth inning to drive in the tying run and set the table for Stephens to be the hero for the day. Roberto Estalella, formerly of the Giants and Philadelphia Athletics, hit his fourth home run in as many games to help spark Vera Cruz.

The sense of having made the wrong decision about his baseball career had not set in for Stephens as yet. He had heard the loud, boisterous Mexican music and the excitement generated by the fans in the stands. He felt at home.

The Mexican League schedule had Vera Cruz's next game set for Thursday in Monterrey, which was a 450-mile trip. Stephens got a feel for the very different pace and lifestyle of baseball in Mexico during the next four days. The quality of the baseball played in Mexico and the ballparks in which it was played left a lot to be desired. Also, the food didn't agree with him, the language was mostly unintelligible, and he became very lonely.

Stephens' second game was against Monterrey. There were no "home crowds" to cheer him on. He went 0-for-4 at the plate and stood at 1-for-8 for the season. That was where his Mexican League campaign would end. In his eight at-bats, he struck out twice and had the one RBI from his first game.

The promises that Jorge Pasquel and others had made and the increased salary suddenly looked unexciting and not worth what the season might hold for him. Life back with the Browns looked to be much more promising and enjoyable.

He had had enough of this quick excursion to Mexico. Now the secret was to find a way to escape. "Escape" was the operative word here, for if the Pasquels became aware of his plan, his life might be in jeopardy. As much as they had welcomed him to their country, there was a sense that they would be as equally displeased if he decided to return to the United States.

Stephens placed a phone call to his father and fortunately was able to make it through the language barrier created by him only speaking English and the Mexican operator being fluent only in Spanish. He arranged a meeting with his father for the following night in Nuevo Laredo. The next challenge was to sneak away from the team in Monterrey and find a way to make the 175-mile trip to Nuevo Laredo without the Pasquels becoming aware of his departure.

He got a ride in a taxicab over poor roads to the rendezvous point. It was a three-and-a-half hour drive to the border. Like most trips in Mexico, it was a fast and dangerous ride, and the passenger's heart was in his throat. He was scared about being stopped along the way and being recognized for who he was. He was also petrified that the driver would go off the road or plow into another vehicle along the way, and he would be killed before his escape was accomplished.

He arrived safely in Nuevo Laredo, and his father and Browns scout Jack Fournier were there to meet him. His next challenge was to get across the International Bridge over the Rio Grande River and safely enter Laredo, Texas.

If the Pasquels had become aware by the time of his escape attempt, they would have had border guards on the lookout for him. Laredo, on the other side of the bridge, wasn't completely safe either, since the Pasquels had established their United States headquarters in the town, from where they concluded much of their of their recruiting.

Stephens quickly changed into his father's clothes and his father donned his. In the hastily produced disguise, Vern walked across the bridge alone and made it safely to the other side. He was free! Stephens' father and Fournier came across the bridge after he arrived on the other side.

Because of his haste to depart from Monterrey, he arrived in Laredo with only the clothes on his father's back. He had left behind what he had brought with him to Mexico, and also some expensive, tailored, double-breasted suits that Jorge Pasquel had presented to his newly arrived star as a welcoming gift.

When commissioner A.B. Chandler lifted the ban on the Mexican jumpers, Vern Stephens was in the midst of an outstanding career with the Boston Red Sox, having been traded from the St. Louis Browns (courtesy Boston Red Sox).

Stephens rejoined the Browns in San Antonio, Texas, and he signed a new contract for more than the $13,000 that the club had originally offered. In that sense, his Mexican excursion had benefited him because it had brought some pressure to bear on Muckerman and DeWitt.

The next day Stephens rejected an increase from Jorge Pasquel that would have raised his annual salary to $25,000 during the five-year period. Pasquel offered to deposit $50,000 of those dollars in a bank in New York City as a guarantee. Stephens did say that he would return the $5,000 advance on his first month's salary that he had received upon his arrival in Mexico and, on April 8, his wife air-mailed a check in that amount to Stephens in care of the St. Louis Browns. Both Stephens and his wife wanted to put the whole affair behind them.

An angry Jorge Pasquel called Sewell and ordered him to bring Stephens back. The Browns' manager would have nothing of it.

Stephens, who said that his contract contained a cancellation clause by which either party could terminate the pact, realized that baseball in the United States was a more reliable option than what he had experienced in Mexico during his short time there.

Stephens offered a personal peeve about an important aspect of baseball in the foreign country, noting, "When you do find a shower, you have to be careful. The tap marked 'C' doesn't mean 'cold,' it means 'hot.' The Mexican word for hot is 'caliente.' The word for cold is 'fria.'"[4]

The Mexican League president and major recruiter was very bitter about the way he had been treated by the erstwhile Vera Cruz shortstop. He told a writer "he would stop at nothing to punish him.... I'm going to get even with him if it is the last thing that I do. I'm going to spend every cent I have to have him extradited to Mexico so that he can be tried here."[5] He also said that he would file a $100,000 suit against the departed player. Pasquel believed that he had the law on his side because Stephens had not signed a 1946 contract with the Browns before he left that club, and he had a signed copy of Stephens' contract to play for the Vera Cruz team in his desk drawer. He did not mention whether or not it had a "cancellation clause" as Stephens claimed that it did.

Because Stephens had returned to the Browns before the "Opening Day deadline" that commissioner "Happy" Chandler had set for those who had gone to Mexico, he was eligible to play for St. Louis in 1946. He would not be subject to the five-year suspension that Chandler had announced for the "outlaw" players.

Stephens went on to have another outstanding season with the Browns. Injuries limited his playing time to 115 games, but he hit a career-high .307 with 14 home runs and 64 RBI. While Gardella and some of the other "jumpers" were playing in the Mexican League All-Star game in Mexico City on July 9, 1946, Stephens was at shortstop for the American Leaguers in their game against the National Leaguers at Fenway Park, Boston. He was the backup to Johnny Pesky of the hometown Red Sox, who himself might have been in Mexico that day if he had been willing to take the Pasquels' offer. After Stephens came into the game, he went 2-for-3, scored a run, had two RBI, and made four flawless plays at shortstop as the American Leaguers crushed their opponents, 12–0.

On August 30, Jorge Pasquel reported that he had received the $5,000 check that Stephens said that he would send shortly after leaving Mexico. Pasquel said that Stephens' check had been addressed incorrectly, and that appeared to be the reason for the delay in its delivery. The Mexican League president added that he would send a check to Stephens for the two games he had played for Vera Cruz early in the season.

Some of the players who had gone to Mexico in 1946 remained there to play in 1947. Those who had returned to the United States were under the five-year suspension that Chandler had put into affect. Some of that group went to Canada to play baseball there.

Stephens, the one who had returned and had protected his career, played for the Browns in 1947 before being traded to the Red Sox in November of that year along with pitchers Ellis Kinder and Jack Kramer. In return, St. Louis received 10 players and $375,000.

His first three seasons with Boston were the best of his career. He smashed 29, 39, and 30 home runs and drove in 137, 159, and 144 runs, with the last two totals leading the American League.

Stephens would have been a gem for the Mexican League had he decided to stay.

◆ 8 ◆

Luis Olmo: A Valuable Dodger Leaves Ebbets Field

Luis Olmo was born in Arecibo, Puerto Rico, on August 11, 1919. The right-handed–hitting outfielder made his debut with the Brooklyn Dodgers on July 23, 1943. He was the first quality player from Puerto Rico to make it to the major leagues.

Olmo was the first Brooklyn player to leave the Dodgers and head to Mexico, departing before the opening of the season. He soon was followed out of the Dodgers' fold by catcher Mickey Owen. Brooklyn, along with the New York Giants, were major targets for the Pasquels.

After opening day, the Pasquels fixed their sights on another Brooklyn player and attempted to lure a number of others to Mexico. In early May, the Mexican brothers sought to sign Stanley Rojek, who had played only one game for Brooklyn in 1942 before heading to military service. Although he was considered a young, highly rated shortstop and a prime prospect in the Brooklyn organization, his contract for the new season was slated to be only $4,500. The Pasquels tempted him by offering him $20,000 down and $8,000 a year with a proviso that he would receive an additional $2,000 yearly in a three-year contract, provided the Pasquel brothers believed that he merited it. There were reports that he had accepted the money from the Pasquels and was heading to Mexico City, but that proved to be incorrect. Rojek, after considering the offer seriously, rejected it.

Pete Reiser, who also had just returned from military duty, was on the Pasquels' wish list, too. He had been with the Dodgers from

1940 through 1942 before going into the military. He had been voted to the National League All-Star team in 1941 and 1942, and he had led the league in batting with a .343 average in 1941. In May, the Pasquels offered Reiser a $50,000 signing bonus in cash with another $50,000 to be put in the bank to pay his salary. Reiser had some concerns about the arrangement and was not willing to sign. Evidently the Pasquels did not satisfy Reiser's concerns and he decided to remain with Brooklyn.

During their May forays into Dodger land, Mexican League representatives approached two other members of the club. Fourth-year pitcher Hal Gregg, whose record had been 18–13 in 1945, was scheduled to make $8,000 or less for the new season, and he was one of those who heard directly or indirectly from the Pasquels. Twelve-year veteran outfielder Augie Galan was also on the Pasquels' list of "desired Dodgers." He and Gregg decided not to take their offers. At one point, Dodger president Branch Rickey was so angered by the presence of Mexican League representatives that he had one of their scouts thrown out of the Dodgers' spring training facility.

The Pasquels also sought to sign some of those in the Dodgers' farm system. Besides Jackie Robinson, they also approached pitcher Jeanne-Pierre Roy. They gave Roy, a prized pitching prospect, a $4,000 advance on his salary even before he had signed a contract with the Mexican League. Roy said Bernardo and Jorge Pasquel had offered him $50,000 to play three years in the Mexican League.

In 1945, Roy had pitched for Montreal of the International League, Brooklyn's top farm club, and had an outstanding 25–11 record. The 25-year-old hurler had worked 293 innings during the season. His only apparent weakness was that he sometimes ran into periods of wildness. Roy had pitched in the Cuban League during the winter, and, after he pitched and won a championship game, he was given an expensive wrist watch by Bernardo Pasquel. In the end, after being courted by the Pasquels, Roy decided to stay with the Dodgers, and Jorge Pasquel was left with trying to recover the $4,000. Roy said that he had tried to give the money back to one of the Mexican League scouts but he had refused to take it. Roy planned to send it to Pasquel so that the matter would be over.

The Dodgers, like other major league clubs, were welcoming back players who had completed their military service. Brooklyn's outfield during the final wartime season had featured Olmo, Goody Rosen, and Dixie Walker. In 1946, Reiser and Carl Furillo were in the Dodgers' spring training camp. Furillo was a promising rookie who would go on to a 15-year major league career, with 12 seasons in Brooklyn and three campaigns in Los Angeles after the club's move west.

Although Olmo had an excellent season in 1945, he expected that Reiser and Furillo would provide tough competition for outfield spots in the new season. Even with the impressive offensive numbers he had put up that season, he was worried about what the new campaign would hold for him in Brooklyn. In 1945, Olmo appeared in 141 games, hit .313 and drove in 110 runs. He banged 27 doubles, 10 home runs, and led the league with 13 triples. In 1943, his first season with the Dodgers, he had hit .303 in 57 games. However the next year, his average dropped to .258 for the 136 games he played.

Olmo had made $6,000 in 1945, and the Dodgers offered his a $500 raise for the following season. Olmo asked the Dodgers for a $10,000 contract, which was quickly turned down. When Jorge Pasquel jumped into Olmo's financial life with a $20,000 offer, the Dodger outfielder began to seriously consider going to Mexico. Olmo's contract in Mexico would eventually be in the neighborhood of $40,000 for three years. He knew that the Pasquels were willing to part with their money because he had been there when they offered Robinson, an unproven black ballplayer, $6,000, and they had the cash in hand.

When Olmo finally decided to take the Pasquels' money and go to Mexico, his defection was not taken lightly by Organized Baseball. Some believe that it was the loss of Olmo, more than any other player, which eventually prompted commissioner Chandler to announce the policy of a five-year suspension for all players who left Organized Baseball for Mexico.

The Dodgers, who had more faith in Olmo than he might have had in himself, took his loss quite seriously. Rickey made it clear that even though Olmo had signed a Mexican League contract that he would welcome him back with the Dodgers. He had received a report that Olmo was in San Juan, Puerto Rico, and that he had reached agreement with one of the Pasquel brothers to go to Mexico. Rickey said that Olmo agreed to fly from Puerto Rico to Miami, Florida, on February 18 to discuss his situation with the Dodgers and to reopen negotiations. Olmo failed to appear in Miami and Brooklyn's president said, "He didn't come to Miami and last Saturday I got one of those 'or else' telegrams from him, telling of his offer from the Mexican League and asking me for my best offer."[1]

Rickey's son, Branch Jr., continued to try to get the outfielder to come back to the Dodgers. He spoke to Olmo on the telephone on February 20, but reported that it was an unsatisfactory conversation. He wanted to make sure that Olmo knew that they wouldn't put him on waivers if he returned. The Rickeys were aware that the outfielder was a valuable commodity and that the Cincinnati Reds and other clubs would probably claim him if he were placed on waivers by the Dodgers.

Rickey Jr. made telephone contact with Olmo and it proved to be very unsatisfactory for him. The telephone line was not clear, and the language barrier between the two men prohibited any resolution of the issues needing resolution.

It was reported that Olmo would be teaming with ex–Giant Gardella in the Vera Cruz outfield. Before he could put on a Blues' uniform, he found that he had been assigned to the Mexico City Reds. However, Olmo would soon be reassigned by Jorge Pasquel to Vera Cruz. That was the way that the Pasquels often handled the rosters of this pair of clubs that they owned, managed (not in the on-the-field sense), and toyed with.

Luis Olmo's departure from Brooklyn to Mexico was a big loss for the Dodgers (courtesy Los Angeles Dodgers).

Olmo was in Mexico in time for the league's opener on March 21. Vera Cruz beat his Mexico City Reds 12–5. The Brooklyn transplant contributed a home run in the losing effort.

Sportswriter Arthur Daley, writing in the April 3 edition of the *New York Times*, assessed the damage that he thought had been done thus far by the raids on Organized Baseball's talent. Daley believed that only three of the players who had left for Mexico were top-flight players. Vern Stephens was one of them, and he already had returned to the St. Louis Browns. Owen and Olmo were the other two. Daley went on to say:

> In nuisance value they have been looming large enough to give American magnates a sharp pain in the neck, but the actual damage they've done has been negligible, unless you want to include the stirring up of feelings of discontent among some of the players and feelings of uneasiness and indignation among the owners.[2]

Early in his time in Mexico, Olmo injured his knee while sliding. The injury kept him out of action for a month, and he was quite lonely without being able to do anything on the baseball field.

He was selected to be a member of the South All-Star team as one of Vera Cruz's representatives for the July 9. He was on the squad with some of his former teammates from the short time that he had been with the Reds. The South team that captured the game, 11–8, included many players who had come from Organized Baseball. There was clearly an attempt by the Pasquels to showcase them in this event.

As the season progressed, Olmo lost much of his excitement and eagerness to play in Mexico. The injury and the loneliness combined to make his time spent south of the border quite disappointing. He had not found the success that had been an important part of his experience in Brooklyn the previous season.

Although he didn't leave the Mexican League when Owen departed on August 5, he did join the former Blues catcher and manager in a request to Chandler on August 8, for reinstatement to Organized Baseball. He, like Owen, hoped to be able to join the Dodgers in the race for the National League pennant. When the appeal was denied, Olmo completed the season in Mexico.

Mexican Raiders in the Major Leagues

Olmo was listed as Luis (Olmo) Rodriguez in Mexican League statistics as they appear in Pedro Treto Cisneros' *The Mexican League*.[3] He played a combined 59 games with Mexico City and Vera Cruz in 1946, hitting .289 and driving in 42 runs. He had 10 doubles and nine home runs, but the injuries that caused him to miss a number of games cut down on his ability to leg out triples. He had only one three-bagger that season. He remained with Vera Cruz for the 1947 campaign, his final season in Mexico. He hit an improved .301 in 102 games. He posted 23 doubles, five triples, and 14 homers while driving in 72 runs in his second season with the Blues.

♦ 9 ♦

Arnold Malcolm "Mickey" Owen: Back and Forth to Mexico

The name "Mickey Owen" is most often associated with his memorable passed ball in the top of the ninth inning of the fourth game of the 1941 World Series against the New York Yankees. The Brooklyn Dodgers were leading the Yankees, 4–3, at that point in the game. A Dodger victory would have evened the series at two games apiece.

The 3–2, two-out pitch from reliever Hugh Casey, which Yankee outfielder Tommy Henrich swung at and missed, got away from Owen, the catcher, and rolled toward the dugout. As Owen chased the ball, Henrich raced to first base. With only one out remaining for the Yanks, they had a runner standing on first base. Joe DiMaggio, Charlie Keller, and Bill Dickey, the next three New York batters, all reached base. Before Brooklyn could register the third out of the inning, the four Yankee base runners had scored. New York had taken a sudden 7–4 lead at Ebbets Field. The home team failed to score in their last at-bat, and the Yankees took a 3–1 lead in the series. They picked up their fourth victory the following day, and they claimed another World Championship.

Owen also could be remembered as a player who "jumped" to Mexico. He had the most confusing and most contentious experience of all of the players who went south of the border.

Owen took full responsibility for the results of both events — the one at Ebbets Field in 1941, and the sojourn to Mexico five years later. Some years later, with the perspective of time and a sense of humor, the catcher commented on the fateful moment when a game-ending third strike caromed off his glove and allowed a Yankee to reach base safely. He wrote, "I look at the photo of the play. I say yep, that's you, ole Mick."[1]

Owen also took responsibility for the decision to go to Mexico in 1946. The ex–Dodger catcher was opposed to Danny Gardella's suit against Organized Baseball for suspending him and other players for breaking contracts and heading to Mexico. Owen made it clear that the players went to Mexico by choice and that the reserve clause was necessary for the continuing success of Organized Baseball.

Owen, who was born in Nixa, Missouri, on April 14, 1916, made his major league debut with the St. Louis Cardinals on May 2, 1937. The 5-foot-10 inch, 190-pound receiver had come up through the Cardinals' extensive farm system that had been designed and overseen by Branch Rickey, who became president of the Dodgers following the 1942 season. Owen was with the Cardinals through the 1940 season when, on December 4, he was traded to the Dodgers for Gus Mancuso, John Pintar, and $65,000.

He was chosen as an All-Star in 1941 and 1942, and he played in those Mid-Summer Classics. The following two years he was chosen to the teams, but he didn't see action in the games.

Owen was inducted into the Navy early in the 1945 campaign and played in only 24 games for Brooklyn, with a .286 average. He was stationed at Sampson Naval Training Center, 12 miles south of Geneva, New York.

Mike Sandlock, who was acquired from the Boston Braves before the 1945 season, did the bulk of the catching that season, appearing in 80 games and hitting .282 for the third-place Dodgers.

Before the start of spring training, Dodger president Rickey tried to end the rumors that were appearing in the print media that had Owen on the trading block. He said that the catcher had not been offered to the Giants, and that no deal was in the offing.

The Dodgers' president went on to say, "I like Owen very much. He will win for you."[2]

The trade rumors continued, and on March 26, St. Louis Cardinals' president Sam Breadon tried to put to rest a report that Owen

9 ♦ Arnold Malcolm "Mickey" Owen

was coming to the Cards for left-handed pitcher Max Lanier. As things later developed, there was irony in the fact that those two players had been linked together during the preseason.

Along with the reports about what was not going to happen with Owen once he was released from his military obligation, there was one that spoke forcefully about what Owen was going to do. On March 12, Jorge Pasquel, speaking from Mexico City, said that the Dodger catcher would be playing for the Mexico City team in 1946, replacing Fermin "Mike" Guerra. Guerra had left Mexico and had rejoined the Washington Senators, and would be playing for them in 1946.

Owen was released from military duty at on March 30, and on April 1, Rickey announced that he had been informed in a letter dated March 28 that his former catcher was joining the Mexican League. Owen said in the letter that would become a player-manager in the league, and that he couldn't stall the Pasquels any longer. Rickey said that earlier he had invited Owen to meet with him on April 2 to discuss details for the upcoming season. Since Rickey had discovered that he was going to be unable to be in Brooklyn that day, he said that his son Branch Rickey, Jr., would be there to meet with Owen. The meeting never took place.

Owen had been working under a three-year contract that was set to expire in 1945, but it had been interrupted by Owen's military service. The contract contained a special clause that said that it would be extended for the full period after his release from military service. His annual salary was thought to have been $12,500. He was to make $15,000 for the third season of the agreement. The Dodgers' president said that the way things had gone, he hadn't even had a chance to talk with Owen about a contract for 1946. There was another bit of unfinished business for the Brooklyn catcher. He had not yet applied for reinstatement to Organized Baseball from the National Defense List, which was a required action on his part following his discharge from the Navy.

The 30-year-old Owen was a hustling veteran of the Brooklyn pennant races of the early 1940's. He was known to be a catcher with whom the team's pitchers liked to work. Dodger manager Leo Durocher tried to make light of Owen's departure and said that he probably

Mexican Raiders in the Major Leagues

wouldn't have gotten much playing time in 1946. Those who knew the makeup of the club felt that Durocher was taking the "company line" or Rickey's line, and he truly believed that the loss of Owen would be a problem for the club. As the season unfolded, the veteran catcher's absence was a major problem. A number of players, including rookies Bruce Edwards and Ferrell Anderson, Sandlock, and Don Padgett, saw time behind the plate. Before the June trading deadline, Brooklyn acquired catcher Stew Hofferth from the Boston Braves to help shore up the position.

On the same day that Rickey made the announcement about Owen's departure, commissioner Chandler, in Venice, Florida, reiterated his ruling about the five-year suspension of those who had jumped their contracts, saying.

On April 2, Owen was in St. Louis, where he signed a Mexican League contract to be the player-manager of the Torreon club. The Pasquels' final offer was an amount that a former Rickey employee would relish. Owen was to receive a $12,500 bonus to sign a five-year contract at $15,000 per year, and the payment of the fifth year's salary was to be made in advance.

Owen told Jorge Pasquel that he had heard that there was concern on the part of some of the players that their money might not be available when paydays came around. Pasquel offered to put Owen's entire five-year salary in a bank as a guarantee. Owen did not feel that would be proper, but he did agree to accept the bonus and an advance on his first year's contract. Although Owen did

Branch Rickey of the Brooklyn Dodgers kept a tight rein on his funds and on his players (courtesy Los Angeles Dodgers).

not reveal how much money the Pasquels were willing to give him to play in their league, the ex–Dodger did say this about the "sweet" deal:

> they have offered me enough in five years to retire on, the first year's salary in cash, plus a $12,500 cash bonus when I sign in the United States before I leave.[3]

Rickey responded to the development by announcing that he was finished with Owen and that he would not have any more to do with him. He said that if Owen did return he would not get any raise in his salary. Besides the financial aspect, the catcher would also be put up for sale or trade.

Owen's arrival in Mexico was much anticipated by the leaders of the league. The ballplayer was looking forward to his new career with much anticipation. Surprisingly, by April 8, Owen had soured on his Mexican League experience and he and his wife Gloria, who had made the trip with him, were back in San Antonio, Texas. He had balked at joining the league as the player-manager of the Torreon team and had left for home. He had followed Vern Stephens down to Mexico with great excitement and expectation and, like the Browns' shortstop, he was back in the United States after spending only a couple of days in the foreign country.

Owen telephoned Rickey from San Antonio and informed him that he wanted to return to

Mickey Owen had a "back-and-forth" experience with the Mexican League in 1946 (courtesy Los Angeles Dodgers).

the Dodgers. Rickey, who was still angry about Owen's sudden departure after his discharge from the Navy, said that he would be willing to meet with him in four or five days and discuss the return. Since Brooklyn wasn't scheduled to open its regular season until April 16, the catcher still believed that he had come back in time to avoid Chandler's suspension edict.

Rickey informed Owen that he would be permitted to make the application for reinstatement from the National Defense List. The Dodgers' president earlier statement that he would only sell or trade Owen should he decide to return was still a possible outcome.

Hoping that Rickey would change the "sell or trade" pronouncement once the two men met in Brooklyn to straighten things out, Owen spoke about what had caused him to return, saying, "I had to do this. I was afraid I might lose too many friends if I didn't, and those friends in Brooklyn mean a lot."[4]

Owen had only good things to say about his short-term contacts with the Pasquels, especially with Alfonso, with whom he had spent the most time. He added that their dreams of providing top-level baseball for the fans in their country was admirable, and that he was sorry that he couldn't be a part of it.

Jorge Pasquel said that it was a sudden three-year contract offer from Rickey that would be worth $20,000 a season, tax free, and not his allegiance to his friends that had lured Owen back to the Dodgers. Rickey quickly denied that any such offer had ever been made to Owen.

Pasquel took a shot at the Dodgers' president after he heard from his brother Alfonso about the deal, saying, "Well, it's the first time Rickey ever paid a player what he was worth. A Mexican taught him the value of his men."[5]

He also took the occasion to chastise Chandler, who, he said, was not fulfilling his duty as commissioner. He added that he didn't believe that Chandler's predecessor, Kenesaw Mountain Landis, would ever have condoned such action.

Jorge Pasquel pointedly criticized Chandler for allowing Stephens and Owen to return to Organized Baseball after having broken contracts with their teams. He also noted that the fans of Mexican baseball would never forgive the pair of players who had broken contracts with them as well.

The temperamental Jorge Pasquel announced that a $100,000 suit would be filed against Owen to go along with the one that he had filed earlier in the same amount against Stephens. The suit was to be filed in St. Louis, because that was where Owen had signed the Mexican League contract — a copy of which Pasquel had in his possession — and where Owen had received a $20,000 cash advance. The advance included a $12,500 signing bonus and $7,500, as it was described in the suit, as one-half payment of Owen's 1946 salary.

Rickey had been a long and tenacious fighter for retention of Organized Baseball's reserve clause:

> Rickey had been the first to understand that the real issue here was Organized Baseball's reserve clause. He'd built the Cardinals and their farm system on the foundation of the clause and had done the same at Brooklyn, and he felt there was a great deal more at stake than the status of Mickey Owen. To take Owen back under any circumstances, he felt, was to equivocate in a matter fundamental to the survival of the game. It was far better, then, to make do at catcher in 1946, with rookies Ferrell Anderson and Bruce Edwards. Probably Rickey ordered his manager to back him up in the Owen matter, because as soon as Rickey spoke, Durocher echoed him saying that it was a matter of no concern where Owen happened to be at the moment: he could go back to Mexico or stay on his farm in Missouri and feed his livestock, Durocher said. He had no plans for Mickey now.[6]

Owen and Rickey never had their meeting. Rickey's threat about trading Owen to another club had continued to ring in the catcher's ears. Unable to hook on with any team in the United States, Owen lingered on his farm waiting for Rickey and Durocher to change their minds and take him back with the Dodgers. After a few days, when that didn't happen, Owen decided to resume his duties in the Mexican League, having been recalled by the Pasquels from Torreon. On April 12, Owen and his wife flew into Mexico City, and he announced that he was back to play baseball.

A smiling and triumphant Jorge Pasquel described Owen's odyssey that had brought him to Mexico City. When the catcher arrived in San Antonio on his way to Mexico, he was mobbed by at least 150 fans who begged him to stay in the United States. The pressure was such that Owen told those in the crowd that he was returning home. Rather than go back to his farm in Missouri, he went to Louisiana and telephoned Pasquel. After the conversation, Pasquel sent his brother Alfonso to Texas, and he met Owen in Houston. Owen and Alfonso went back to Laredo and spent the night at Alfonso's home. In the morning they took a flight from Laredo to Mexico City. There wasn't an announcement yet about where Owen would play. Perhaps he would still be in Torreon, but he also could be with Vera Cruz. The Blues had lost their catcher Chico Hernandez, who had come from the Chicago Cubs in 1944, with a broken ankle. He had returned to his Havana, Cuba, home.

Rickey expressed surprise when he heard that Owen had changed his mind again and was back in Mexico. He commented:

> I can't understand the young man. Last Tuesday it was he who took the initiative and phoned me from San Antonio, saying he had gone too far toward Mexico already, that he was anxious to return to the Dodgers.[7]

Owen attended a game between Mexico City and San Luis Potosi the day after his arrival in Mexico City. Before 20,000 cheering fans, it was announced that he would be behind the plate the following day in the game against the Monterrey Sultans, wearing a Blues uniform. An exuberant Jorge Pasquel witnessed the explosion of excitement in the stadium.

The new Vera Cruz catcher's contract, which contained a salary increase for being the Blues' player-manager, included an interesting appendage. He would only be a player in 1946, and would then add the job of managing the club the following season. Ramon Bragana, a Cuban Negro who had pitched in the league since 1938 and had been with Vera Cruz since 1940, would continue in the dual role as player-manager until 1947.

Owen and his wife moved into an apartment in a nice section of Mexico City, and the catcher spoke in a positive manner about how well he was being taken care of by the Pasquels. On April 16, even as Chandler's suspension edict went into effect, Owen displayed satisfaction abut what his future in Mexico looked like.

The Vera Cruz catcher also was impressed with how the league was being run. He said that because 75 percent of the gate receipts were being pooled in a common fund, that he was going to play in the most democratic league in the world.

The "player-only" arrangement did not last long, and soon Owen was managing the club. He had the team with the highest payroll and with the largest number of imports from the United States, and the Blues were languishing at or near the bottom of the league. The people in Mexico City, where the transplanted Blues played their home games, were expecting much more from this collection of players.

Vera Cruz's pitching staff was not strong. A three-man staff was sufficient in the Mexican League because of the limited schedule played by the teams. The 37-year-old Bragana was the leader of the staff. Right-hander Alex Carrasquel, who had come south from the Washington Senators in 1946, was the number two starter, and 19-year-old Rodriguez "Tito" Herrera was the third pitcher in the rotation. Reliever "Schoolboy" Johnny Taylor completed the staff.

As Owen's season progressed, he became unhappy with the makeup of the staff, and it did not have to do mainly with the quality of the pitchers. It had to do with the skin color of some of them. He complained to Jorge Pasquel and told him that he didn't catch any Negroes. They were not part of major league baseball in the United States, and he didn't want them to be a part of his game in Mexico. Soon there were changes on Vera Cruz's roster, and most of the non-white players were moved to other clubs. Carrasquel, who was a native of Venzuela, and who had been welcome in Washington with the Senators, was dispatched to the Mexico City team, and Taylor was sent to San Luis Potosi. Max Lanier, a recent "jumper" from the St. Louis Cardinals, joined the Blues' staff. Some noted that the Blues' name should be changed to the Vera Cruz "Whites."

Owen became a "league ambassador" while he was with Vera Cruz. He was part of a two-man delegation from the Mexican League that went to see Stan Musial when he returned to St. Louis with the team

Mexican Raiders in the Major Leagues

on June 1. Alfonso Pasquel and Owen paid a visit to the Cardinals' star at the Fairgrounds Hotel, where he was living with his wife and infant son. At the time Musial was making $13,500 with the Cards. Musial was offered a $65,000 bonus in cashier's checks for signing a contract with the Mexican League. Owen told him that Jorge Pasquel was having a house built for himself, and he gave the impression that the same would be available for the Cardinals' All-Star, who was living the "hotel life" at the time.

Musial thought about the enticing offer:

> Here was a hard sell, but Musial, though he was one of the most genial, affable men in the big leagues, was also a fairly shrewd negotiator. He'd been raised in a tough town that turned out nails and wire, and he'd learned early in life the value of a dollar earned. He told his visitors he couldn't make so momentous a decision on the spot, but he would have to think it through with his wife.[8]

After talking the offer over with his wife that evening, he informed Alfonso Pasquel that he was going to honor his 1946 contract with the Cardinals. However, Pasquel had the sense that it was not a dead issue for the future.

In an interesting aftermath to the Pasquel and Owen visit, the Musials "found housing" shortly thereafter, and moved out of the hotel and into a private home.

Owen was chosen to be the starting catcher for the South team in the All-Star Game on July 9. Bookers "Balazos" McDaniels, the ace of the San Luis Potosi staff, was also an All-Star, and he was named to be the South's starter against the North squad. McDaniels had been born in Morrilton, Arizona, and he was a Negro.

Before the start of the game, Owen and Ernesto Carmona, the manager of the South squad, were embroiled in a heated argument. Owen was telling Carmona that he would not catch McDaniels, and Carmona was telling Owen that if he didn't he would be sent to jail for a breach of contract. After the umpire yelled "Play Ball," Owen headed to his position behind home plate

The North team scored a pair of runs off McDaniels in the top of the first inning, but he settled down and didn't surrender a run in the following pair of innings. The North squad had some hard hit drives that were right at the South's fielders. It was a surprise to some that San Luis Potosi's fireballing pitcher failed to strike out a single batter during his three innings of work. He was leading the Mexican League in strikeouts at the time. There was a suggestion that Owen had been telling some of the North's hitters what pitches were coming and they were ready for him.

As the season progressed, Owen did not impress many of the locals with his offensive output. He battled at the plate, and he failed to deliver in a manner that, in the opinion of other players and fans, justified the large salary that he was being paid by the Pasquels. At times, he benched himself when he was in the midst of an extended hitting slump.

He also battled on the field. He was in several altercations with umpires and players on the other clubs. In June, a game between Vera Cruz and Mexico City was held up for almost an hour, and Owen, who was the major combatant, was banished by umpire Amado Maestri for his role in the melee. Jorge Pasquel came out of the stands in an effort to help quell the disturbance. In a game a short time later, Owen was in an on-the-field fight with Monterrey outfielder Claro Duany, a Cuban Negro, who was leading the Mexican League in hitting at the time. Duany was attempting to score from second base on a single to left-center field. The throw home arrived in Owen's glove with time to spare, and the fleet-footed Cuban smashed into the Blues' catcher, trying to dislodge the ball. The two players went at each other, and soon a brawl between many of the players on both teams was taking place. When peace was restored, both players were ejected from the game. They also were suspended for a week for being in the fracas.

On another occasion, Owen believed that the umpire, who was a Cuban, had missed a close play at the plate. The enraged Owen rushed toward the umpire to give him a piece of his mind. Bobby Estalella, another former player from Organized Baseball, gave Owen a warning and perhaps saved him from a painful experience. Estalella said, "Don't go too close, Mickey. He'll crack you over the head with his mask."[9]

Jorge Pasquel rushed onto the field to support and protect Owen and bring an end to the dispute. The umpire threatened to attack

Pasquel with his mask, and Jorge's bodyguard pulled a knife to send a message to the "man in blue." The umpire left the field and, by sundown, he was out of the country.

Owen left Mexico for the second time that season on August 5. Once again, he had become disillusioned by what he was going though. He had three specific complaints about his time in Mexico. First, he had signed a contract to manage and catch for the Torreon club, which he had preferred to do, and that never happened. He claimed that he had been fired from the Torreon position, and that effectively had ended his contract. Next, the Pasquels sent him to play for Vera Cruz and, finally, while he was there, they had converted him to a first baseman, a position he had never played. He also added some additional complaints that had been heard from other players: the altitude; the food; and the playing conditions in the ballparks.

Owen appeared in 51 games for the Blues and batted .256. He went to the plate 203 times and produced 52 hits and had 25 RBI. He added six doubles, three triples, and three home runs to his modest offensive output.

Not only was Owen disillusioned, he was also quite naïve, because he thought that he could return to Organized Baseball and rejoin the Dodgers in their National League pennant fight with the Cardinals.

Owen made his way by train to Cincinnati where he hoped to meet with Chandler and plead his case for his reinstatement. He reasoned that he had never been reinstated afer he had left the service and therefore he had not broken his contracts with the Dodgers.

Owen did not believe that he had failed to meet his obligation to the Pasquels and to the Mexican League, and therefore he owned them nothing.

Chandler was not in Cincinnati when Owen arrived, having gone to his home in Versailles, Kentucky, for the weekend. The commissioner had arranged for him to meet with his assistant Herold "Muddy" Ruel, a 19-year American League catcher who had retired in 1934. After a one hour and 45-minute meeting, Ruel said that he would turn over his findings to Chandler, who would have the final say in the matter. He did remind Owen, however, about the law that stated that no player who is on the voluntary retired list or who is ineligible may be reinstated during the period from August 1 to October 1 during the playing year. Putting the Mexican journey aside, it looked as if Owen's hope to play in 1946 was not very probable.

Rickey appeared to have modified his stance on the Owen situation and said that he would be willing to help him in any way that he could. Branch Jr., who was the club's vice president, was more specific, saying, "Certainly we want him. We hold nothing against Mickey and now it is up to the commissioner to decide whether he can have another chance."[10] Perhaps the reason for the Rickeys' change in attitude had something to do with the struggles the team had experienced trying to replace Owen behind the plate. At the time of Owen's return, Brooklyn was 62–40 and held a slim two-game lead over St. Louis in the National League's exciting pennant race.

It didn't take long for other major league players to register their opinions about Owen's hope to return to action in 1946 — and the vast majority of those who spoke up were opposed to Chandler allowing him to play again that season.

The Philadelphia Phillies voted unanimously that Owen should be suspended for the five years that was announced by the commissioner in his ruling. They felt that it would be unfair to other players if he were allowed to return to active states.

Marty Marion, the veteran All-Star shortstop for the Cardinals and a former teammate of Owen with the team in 1940, along with Cards' left-handed pitcher Howie Pollet were also on the side of not allowing Owen to return. They felt the same way about Hal Lanier, the Cards' southpaw, who had also gone to Mexico.

George McQuinn, the Philadelphia Athletics' first baseman, was not quite as adamant about upholding the suspension as most others. He suggested that Owen shouldn't be allowed to play this year, but maybe he and the others who had jumped could come back and play next year. Dizzy Trout, a pitcher with the Detroit Tigers, also advocated the possibility of a shorter suspension for those who wanted to return to Organized Baseball.

It had been reported that the Yankee players would go on strike if Chandler gave Owen the go-ahead to return to the Dodgers, but, on August 7, Dickey, the Yanks' manager, said that was not the case.

However, in Jersey City, New Jersey, Charles Stoneham, secretary of the New York Giants' farm club there, said his club was willing to forfeit one game as a protest if Chandler approved Owen's request to be reinstated.

Dodgers' outfielder Augie Galan, the team's representative in the player-owner conferences, noted that Owen's jump to Mexico had helped to start the money flowing, and a number of players on the Giants and Dodgers had received raises.

Chandler announced his decision in the Owen case on August 14. The commissioner ruled that Owen must pay the full penalty of the five-year suspension from Organized Baseball. He clarified one point of Owen's disagreement with the baseball ruling. Chandler said the catcher had been suspended on May 9 for leaving the Dodgers. So, in fact, Owen had been included on the list of all of those who had jumped their teams' contracts to follow the Pasquels' money.

Owen accepted the ruling and headed to his farm in Springfield, Missouri. He was not going back to Mexico for a third time. He didn't need any more of Mexican League baseball.

He listed these problems with the operation of the league:

> The Mexican League wasn't a major league ... and it never would be as long as (Jorge) Pasquel insisted on running it as his private plaything, hiring and firing managers at whim, arranging phony player trades, even interrupting games to order pitching changes or argue with an umpire's decision.[11]

A few days after his appeal was denied, Owen announced that he would make a second appeal to Chandler and ask him to reconsider the ruling. The second appeal did not produce a different result from the first. At 30 years of age, the five-year suspension was not going to leave Owen with many more good years to play the game.

The flurry of activity around Owen brought Jorge Pasquel back into the limelight. Upon hearing about Chandler's refusal to lift the ban on Owen, he said he felt better about the resolution of the Owen affair.

Over the ensuing days, Jorge Pasquel made an announcement that was aimed at Owen and the game North of the Border. He said that

9 ♦ *Arnold Malcolm "Mickey" Owen*

because of the actions of the ex–Vera Cruz catcher, he was redoubling his efforts to encourage the top players in the majors to come to Mexico and accept the large salaries the league was able to offer.

Jorge Pasquel also announced that he was suing Owen for $127,500, and that suit was filed in Federal District Court in Springfield, Missouri, on August 28. He was asking for the return of the $12,500 bonus that had been paid to Owen for deserting the Dodgers after he left military service and for the money that he had been paid in advance as salary for the 1950 season, the final year of his contract. The suit also asked for an additional $100,000 in damages from Owen.

Owen spent the remainder of the summer working on his farm. He also hooked on as a catcher with the town's softball team.

◆ 10 ◆

George Hausmann, Sal Maglie, and Roy Zimmerman: Three More Giants Head South

At the end of March, the Pasquel brothers raided the New York Giants for a second time when they signed regular second baseman George Hausmann, right-handed pitcher Salvatore Maglie, and back-up first baseman Roy Zimmerman to Mexican League contracts. On February 19, Danny Gardella had become the first Giant player to sign a contract to play in the Mexican League.

After signing to play in the Mexican League, Gardella became a recruiter for the Pasquels, and he attempted to interest Hausmann, Maglie, and Zimmerman in joining him on the trip south. He told them about the financial opportunities that awaited them. At the time, none of the three Giants was ready to make the move. They appeared to still be committed to staying and playing for the Polo Grounders.

On March 31, after a heavy downpour of rain had washed out the final two spring training exhibition games that were scheduled against the Philadelphia Phillies, manager Mel Ott, who had not been disappointed by the loss of Gardella, received news that he had lost the three players, including Hausmann, who was expected to be the team's starting second baseman. They had signed Mexican League contracts the previous day. Ott had become increasingly more agitated by the prospect of losing more of his players to the Mexican League. His agitation appeared to have led to accusations about some of the players' commitments to the Giants, and that had led to the three players' decisions to leave the club.

Mexican Raiders in the Major Leagues

Although the three players expected to be on the same Mexican League team, they would be sent to different clubs. Hausmann spent the season with Torreon, Maglie was with Puebla, and Zimmerman played for Nuevo Laredo.

Horace C. Stoneham, the president of the club, immediately informed the trio that they had been suspended and that they would no longer be receiving Giants paychecks. The players believed that they were now in a position where their next paychecks from their new teams would be much larger than the ones they would have received from New York. Each of the players said they had received a $5,000 bonus for signing and that they would be receiving an additional $1,000 for expenses. It was thought at the time that Hausmann had signed with the Giants for $8,500 in 1946. Maglie estimated that the players would receive at least twice as much as they would have received from the Giants.

Stoneham, after suspending the three players, said, "We are well-pleased the way things turned out. So long as they wanted to go to Mexico the quicker they went the better. We no longer have any use for them."[1]

Hausmann was born in St. Louis, Missouri, on February 11, 1916. He had come to the Giants from their minor league club in New Orleans, Louisiana, for the 1944 season. In spring training, the diminutive 5'5", 145-pounder beat out Hugh Luby, a Pacific Coast League favorite, who did not like the cold weather and asked Ott to train in California. By the time Luby joined the Giants, Hausmann had won the second base job.

Hausmann was a regular on Ott's wartime teams, playing in 131 games in 1944. He hit .266 for the Giants, who finished in fifth place in the National League, 38 games behind the pennant-winning St, Louis Cardinals. In 1945, he was at second base in all of the fifth-place club's 154 games, and he raised his batting average to .279. In 1946, Hausmann was battling rookie Buddy Blattner for second, but, at the time of his departure, it looked as if he would hold on to the position.

Maglie was born in Niagara Falls, New York, on April 26, 1917. The 6'2", 180-pound right-hander had played in the minors before the war, but he had not posted impressive records. He left baseball in 1942 and took a job at a defense plant.

10 ♦ George Hausmann, Sal Maglie, and Roy Zimmerman

George Hausmann was in line to be the New York Giants' second baseman when he jumped to the Mexican League (National Baseball Hall of Fame Library, Cooperstown, N.Y.).

Maglie received an offer from the Giants to join their minor league club in Jersey City, New Jersey, for the 1945 season. He benefited, like many other players at the time, from the shortage of players caused by the war, and he was called to New York late in the season even though he had struggled to a 3–7 record with Jersey City. Maglie made his major league debut on August 9. The 28-year-old rookie appeared in 13 games for the Giants after his callup, posting a 5–4 record, with a 2.35 ERA and three shutouts. Seven of his 10 starts were complete-game outings.

Zimmerman was born in Pine Grove, Pennsylvania, on September 13, 1916. He was obtained from Newark late in 1945 when the Giants needed help at first base. He made his major league debut on September 2. The 6'2", 187-pound left-hander was at first base in 27 games and hit .276 after joining the Giants. With the return of veteran Johnny Mize from military service, it didn't appear as if Zimmerman would be getting much playing time in New York in 1946.

Maglie had a non-guaranteed $7,500 contract with the Giants for 1946, but he didn't know how much a part of the pitching staff he would be. During spring training he was housed in the same second-class hotel where Gardella had stayed during his short time at the camp. The fact that he wasn't in the best housing gave him a message that his spot on the club was precarious.

Ott, who was aware that Maglie had been an effective pitcher in the Cuban League during the winter, had been encouraging to him at the start of the training camp. However, the right-hander didn't feel that he was really near the top of Ott's pitching list for the upcoming season although he had some strong outings early in the training camp, including striking out seven batters in five innings of an intrasquad game.

When the exhibition season began, the manager didn't give him much work. Maglie would not make the $7,500 if he was returned to Jersey City, and he believed that might happen. When he left New York's training camp, there were still 25 pitchers there vying for spots on the Giants' regular season roster.

Of all the players who went to Mexico to play baseball, Maglie was the one who gained the most from his time south of the border. Adolfo Luque was the person most responsible for turning the Giant with a 5–4 major league record into an outstanding Mexican League pitcher and later, after Chandler's suspension was lifted, a top pitcher in the majors who ended his career with a 119–62 mark.

Luque, a native of Havana, Cuba, had pitched in the National League with several clubs from 1915 until 1935. He appeared in two games of the ill-fated 1919 World Series that pitted the Chicago White Sox against the Cincinnati Reds. Luque pitched a total of five shutout innings in two games for the Reds, giving up only one hit and striking out six in five innings. He finished his career with a 194–179 record. The right-hander's best season was 1923, when he went 27–8 with the league runner-up Reds. He was the Giants' pitching coach from 1935–1938 and from 1941–1945.

Luque had a hand in Maglie's early development during their short time together in 1945 with the Giants. However, his greatest impact on the right-hander would come later during the time they were together in the Mexican League.

In 1945, the pitching coach convinced a hesitant Ott to put Maglie in the Giants' rotation after his arrival from Jersey City. He also lined Maglie up to pitch for the Cienfuegos club in the Cuban League following the 1945 season. Luque was there as well, and he continued to work with Maglie as he had done during the later part of the Giants' regular season. It was then that Maglie began to have the success that he would experience during most of the rest of his career.

The goal of Luque's tutelage was to change Maglie's "flat curveball" into a sharp-breaking curveball that would handcuff the batter. The pitching coach had learned to throw his own devastating curveball through instructions from the great Christy Mathewson.

Luque managed the Cienfuegos team in the Cuban League during the winter, and he signed Maglie to pitch for the club. As the tutoring continued, the pupil began to display significant success. By the end of the season he was turning the heads of the fans throughout the loop. He beat the Havana Reds, the league's premier club, all seven times that he faced them, including shutting them out in the championship game. After tasting success during the winter season, he realized that he might not know that feeling again in the majors with the talent-laden Giants. Ott had followed Maglie's pitching in the winter league in Cuba, but it was not impressive enough to put him at the top of the heap in the Giants' 1946 spring training camp.

Jorge Pasquel talked with Maglie in Cuba about taking his talents to Mexico and playing there. Pasquel described what he had in store for players during the coming season, and he thought that the right-handed pitcher would be a welcome addition to his league. Later, Hausmann and Zimmerman made contact with Bernardo Pasquel to talk about the opportunity that had been introduced to Maglie. They both knew about the competition that awaited them in spring training. The timing was not quite right for the trio, and they looked forward to spring training with the Giants.

When Maglie arrived in the Giants' training camp, Luque was no longer on the staff. He had become the manager for Puebla in the Mexican League. That was where Maglie ended up, and the tutoring continued. Although Luque's departure from the Giants was not enough to make Maglie head for the Mexican League, it became an option worth considering when he became discouraged about his major league future during spring training. When he left for Mexico he didn't know which team he would be with and who his manager would be.

He and Luque teamed up in Puebla with the Parrots. Puebla was the third largest city in the league with a population of 137,327 people. The playing field was a flat piece of arid land that had a fence around it. It was judged to be one of the poorest fields in the league.

Besides working on his curveball, Luque helped Maglie develop a "persona" that would hold him in good stead throughout his playing days. Maglie had an ever-present "five o'clock shadow" which betrayed his nickname as "the Barber." Luque taught him to use his fastball to claim the inside part of the plate as his own. He would "shave" a batter with the high, inside, hard one to drive them off the plate and to take away any degree of comfort they might have when they faced the aggressive right-hander.

Puebla was a team without any Americans other than Maglie. The fact that Jorge Pasquel had not assigned him to Vera Cruz, Mexico City, or Torreon, each of which he and his brothers owned or had a controlling financial interest in, sent a message that the Pasquels didn't expect him to be a dominant pitcher in the league. Hausmann's assignment with Torreon placed him at a level above Maglie in the Pasquels' mind. Zimmerman, who was with Nuevo Laredo, appeared to be at the same level of expectation as Maglie.

Puebla club owner Castor Montoto knew that his club had limited financial resources, and he told Jorge Pasquel that he would not be able to pay more than one "high-priced" American import. On April 13, the day before Maglie's arrival, Montoto estimated that the pitcher's $10,000 salary would be a huge drain on the club's $80,000 gate receipts for the season. There didn't appear to be any way that he would make money in 1946.

Napoleon Reyes and Adrian Zabala were the two other players with Puebla who had come from Organized Baseball, but they were Cubans and didn't count as American acquisitions. Both had been with the Giants before coming to Mexico.

Maglie had a very successful season in 1946, but he also experienced some conditions that had made his time in Mexico far different from what it had been in the United States. The team did most of its traveling in and out of Puebla by bus over the mountains. The buses were often driven over the narrow, winding roads by madmen.

Puebla battled in the middle of the league's standings during the year. However, Maglie was at the top of the league in what he accomplished on the mounds throughout the circuit. His 285⅓ innings pitched placed him fifth all time in that category in the history of the Mexican League. He appeared in 47 games with the Parrots, winning 20 and losing 12.

He had been transformed by working with Luque. His flat curveball had become an impressive weapon that often seemed to take the bat out of the hands of the overmatched hitter.

Hausmann had a productive season playing for Torreon. He hit .306 in 90 games, and his speed helped him leg out a league-leading 15 triples.

He was with the Monterrey Sultans in 1947 where he batted .278 in 116 games. He was out of the Mexican League the following season, but he reappeared with Nuevo Laredo at the start of the 1949 season. He only played in 27 games and hit .223 before heading back to the United States to resume his major league career.

Zimmerman appeared in 83 games for Nuevo Laredo in 1946, hitting .255. That was the end of his professional career. He was not in the Mexican League in 1947 and did not play Organized Baseball when the ban was lifted in 1949.

Maglie was back with Puebla in 1947, and he had another banner season. He was a 20-game winner for the second season in a row. Appearing in 39 games, he lost 13 times and posted a 3.92 ERA.

♦ 11 ♦

Lou Klein, Max Lanier, and Fred Martin: The St. Louis Cardinal Jumpers

The Brooklyn Dodgers and the New York Giants were the first teams to lose players to the Mexican League. The Pasquels believed that they had the financial resources available to make their offers quite appealing to underpaid players on other teams in Organized Baseball.

The Dodgers and the Giants had watched some of their players depart during the 1946 spring training. The St. Louis Cardinals didn't lose any of their players until the regular season was under way.

On May 23, pitchers Max Lanier and Freddie Martin and infielder Lou Klein failed to report for a Cardinals game against the Giants at the Polo Grounds in New York. There was talk that they had accepted money from the Pasquels and were on their way to Mexico. It was the second time that the Pasquels had made a successful three-player raid on Organized Baseball, having signed George Hausmann, Sal Maglie, and Roy Zimmerman, all of the Giants, on March 30.

Before the season, in one poll, the Cardinals were chosen by 115 out of 119 baseball writers to finish at the top of the National League. The other four writers voted for the Chicago Cubs, who had captured the pennant in 1945. The National League's managers, in another survey, all selected the Cards to finish in first place. Klein, Lanier, and Martin were seen as important players on this possibly pennant-bound club.

While a number of the players from other teams who had jumped to Mexico, like Danny Gardella and Mickey Owen, had not signed contracts for 1946 and were being held by baseball's reserve clause, the St. Louis trio were playing the season under a contract that they had signed for 1946.

After the series finale against the Giants on May 23, second baseman Red Schoendienst returned to the hotel room in New York he was sharing with Lanier and found that his roommate's luggage was gone. He also discovered a note on the bureau that read, "So long, Red. Keep hitting those line drives. I'll see you next winter, and we'll go hunting."[1]

Klein and Martin had returned from the service for the 1946 season. Klein, who was a native of New Orleans, Louisiana, had been the Cardinals' regular second baseman in 1943 and hit .287. He played every inning of every game that season. After losing almost two years of baseball while serving in military service, the 5'11", 170-pound infielder was in a battle with Schoendienst for the second base job during spring training.

Whitey Kurowski had been a holdout early in spring training and, during that period, the Cards' new manager, Eddie Dyer, moved Schoendienst to Kurowski's spot at third base and Klein was inserted as the second baseman.

Kurowski was another player whom the Pasquels wanted to attract to Mexico, and they made him a sizeable offer to leave the Cards. Finally, on May 4, the Cardinal infielder rejected the $100,000 contract offer and $20,000 signing bonus to remain in St. Louis. When Kurowski signed and assured the Cardinals that he was not heading for Mexico, Dyer sent him back to third base, where he had played as a regular for the Cards since 1942. That put the younger and quicker Schoendienst at second. By mid–May, it had become clear to Klein that he was not going to be anything other than a utility infielder.

Martin was born in Williams, Oklahoma, and, in 1946, he was a 31-year-old rookie right-handed pitcher. He had been in the Cardinals' expansive minor league system since 1935, and he had not opened many eyes with his performance until 1941. That season, with Dyer as his minor league manager, he began to use a sinker and he fashioned an outstanding 23–6 record with an impressive 1.52 earned-run average. As was happening for other players, Martin was soon leaving for military service. He was one of the first ballplayers to enter military

11 ♦ Lou Klein, Max Lanier, and Fred Martin

Lou Klein decided to leave for Mexico after it looked as if he would have a backup role with the St. Louis Cardinals (National Baseball Hall of Fame Library, Cooperstown, N.Y.).

service, and he was one of the last to be discharged. When he returned, he was joining a deep and talented club. He performed well during spring training, but as the season approached there were questions as to how Dyer would use him in the club's rotation.

Klein and Martin had both played ball in Cuba during the winter in an effort to prepare themselves for the challenges of the first postwar season. While there, they were approached by Mexican League scouts and were told of the opportunities that awaited them in the Mexican League. Even before spring training, Martin was mentioned as someone who might be interested in going to Mexico.

Bernardo Pasquel also made an offer to Lanier while the Cards were in Philadelphia from May 19 to May 21 for a series against the Phillies. The 5'7", 187-pound left-handed Lanier, who was a native of Denton, North Carolina, had been with the Cardinals since 1938, and he had gone 10–8, 13–8, 15–7, and 17–12 from 1941 through 1944. He was the top winning left-hander on the Cards' pennant-winning clubs from 1942 to 1944.

Throughout his career with the Cardinals, Lanier had battled president Sam Breadon and other members of the Cardinal management about their approaches to personnel issues and salaries. In 1934, shortly after he was signed by the club, Lanier quit because he was not sent to the minor league team that he was told that he would be with. The Cardinals re-signed him two years later because they still considered him to be a valuable prospect.

Lanier had argued about contract amounts throughout his time with the major league club. After his 17–12 record and a 2.65 ERA in 1944 with the World Champion Cardinals, when he made $10,000, he went into the military. Upon his return for the 1946 campaign, his contract called for him to make the same amount as in 1944. He arrived at spring training without having signed a contract. Lanier was not in the mood to do his pitching for $10,000. Dyer spoke to Breadon on Lanier's behalf and told the tight-fisted president that he thought that the pitcher was due a raise. Breadon increased Lanier's salary by $500 and told him to take it or leave it. Lanier took it but was not happy about the resolution of his complaint. The "leaving it" would come a short time later.

11 ♦ Lou Klein, Max Lanier, and Fred Martin

Lanier was not the only St. Louis player who, over the years, had been dissatisfied by the amount of money that was offered in a contract. There had been a history of Cardinal players who felt that they had been short-changed. Before going to the Dodgers following the 1942 season, general manager Branch Rickey had been the Cards' chief determiner of players' salaries. Breadon entered the discussions only when the two sides were at a standstill and the team's president proved to be a tough negotiator and was never willing to give an inch.

When Lanier came back to the Cardinals in 1946 after his military service, he brought a sore arm back with him. He attributed the arm injury to an outing against a team of major leaguers while he was at Ft. Bragg, North Carolina. He had not thrown for awhile before going to the mound for the outing, and he said that he hurt his arm in the game.

Lanier struggled during spring training, and the lefty took the injury with him into the regular season. In his outing against the Phillies just before leaving for Mexico, the pain was excruciating, especially when he threw his curveball, and he knew that his arm wasn't getting better. He was afraid to let Dyer and Breadon know about the in injury. He was fearful that if Breadon found out that he was having arm trouble he might be traded or released. A clause in the Uniform Player's Contract provided for the release of a player provided that he was given a ten-day notice. That meant that in ten days he could be without a job and without a salary.

Breadon was known to be the consummate baseball businessman, and he often treated his players as pieces to be used in the most pragmatic fashion in the business game. The reason for the recent sale of catcher Walker Cooper, who had been with the Cards since 1940, was something that many of the Cardinals failed to comprehend. Cooper, who had been unexpectedly sold to the Giants for $175,000 before he was released from the Navy, had been a good-hitting receiver before going into the military. He had fashioned a .318 average in 122 games in 1943 and finished second to teammate Stan Musial in the balloting for the Most Valuable Player that year. The following season he continued to excel at the plate, hitting .317. Cooper was voted to the National League's All-Star team in 1942, 1943, and 1944.

Lanier's arm problems were not evident in the way he began the 1946 season. He might have been pitching with pain, but he was also pitching with success. He had six starts for the Cardinals, winning each game and going the distance in each outing. In the second game of the season, he shut out the Pittsburgh Pirates, 6–0, and he followed that with a 4–1 win over Cincinnati. Lanier beat Chicago, 4–0, and Boston, 7–2, in his next two complete-game performances. He topped Brooklyn, 7–5, in his fifth start, and handled Philadelphia, 9–5, in his most painful outing to bring his season's record to 6–0.

The Pasquels sweetened their offer to Klein, and he accepted it. Martin already had received $3,000 as a bonus for reporting to Mexico.

Bernardo Pasquel's offer to Lanier in Philadelphia gave the Cardinal pitcher a way to avoid letting the Cardinals know about this arm injury as well as a way to get paid while suffering through the discomfort. On the morning of May 23, after meeting with Bernardo Pasquel at the Roosevelt Hotel in New York City, he finally agreed to join Klein and Martin and go to Mexico. Each of the players received their signing bonuses from the stash of $100 bills that the Mexican League official had in his suitcase. A report said that the sore-armed Lanier received a $50,000 signing bonus and his contract would be for five years with a salary of $20,000 the first season.

Breadon, upon hearing about the players' departure, said, "Everyone in baseball knows they are good players. Lanier is the best pitcher in the league, and there is bound to be an effect on the club."[2] He also spoke about the final conversation he had with Lanier and Martin on the telephone when he told the two players that he thought they were making a mistake and would regret their decisions to leave the Cardinals. He noted "they did not ask me anything to indicate they wanted me to offer them new contracts or anything like that. Nor did I bring it up."[3]

Breadon, in an effort to ward off other defections, gave Musial, Enos Slaughter, and Terry Moore substantial bonuses.

Dyer said that he would be willing to take all three of the players back if they returned soon and if Breadon agreed to have them back.

A national rail strike that began on May 23 when 250,000 union

11 ♦ Lou Klein, Max Lanier, and Fred Martin

members left their jobs played havoc with the trio's plans to make it to Mexico City. Klein headed to New Orleans by bus to pick up his belongings and would go to Mexico from there. Lanier and Martin took a bus to Washington, D.C, and were then able to make it to Chicago on one of the few trains that was still running. Jorge Pasquel caught up with them by telephone in Chicago and told the two to take a cab to Mexico City at his expense — for more than $300 in fare.

When the trio left the Cardinals, the team had a 19–10 record and were in a flat-footed tie with the Dodgers. The Cards went 4–7 in their next 11 games and fell into second place. They had a back-and-forth battle with the Dodgers throughout the campaign before capturing the pennant at season's end. St. Louis took the World Series against the Boston Red Sox that was capped by Slaughter's "mad dash" home in the seventh and deciding game.

Lanier, who was considered by many to be the top pitcher on the Cardinals staff, took his 6–0 record and 1.93 earned run average (ERA) with him to the Vera Cruz Blues. Martin had gone 2–1 with a 4.08 ERA in three starts with two complete games before bolting for Mexico, where he joined the Mexico City Reds. Klein had appeared in 23 games with a .194 batting average for the Cardinals, and he was going to be joining the Vera Cruz club.

Klein, Lanier, and Martin were added to Chandler's "banished" list on June 15, and they would not be eligible for reinstatement in Organized Baseball for five years.

Lanier had made his debut with Vera Cruz on June 2, giving up one hit in 3⅔ innings of relief pitching. He also had a single in the top of the 12th inning that started the rally that led to the Blues' 11–9 win over the Reds. Klein was at shortstop for Vera Cruz, and he contributed a pair of hits and two runs to the Vera Cruz victory. Martin appeared in a relief role for Mexico City, surrendering two hits in three innings of work.

The game was put on hold for nearly an hour by a dispute that eventually led to the banishment of Owen by umpire Amado Maestri. Jorge Pasquel, who owned both clubs, came out of the stands in attempt to quell the disturbance but, he too, was banished from the field by Maestri.

Following the Blues' victory, they held a 13–20 record and were in seventh place in the eight-team league. The Reds were 18–15 and sat in third place.

While the Vera Cruz team, with the largest number of imports from Organized Baseball, continued to struggle and disappoint Jorge Pasquel, Lanier and Klein were two of the bright spots on the club. Klein's batting average was among the league's leaders. Lanier continued his winning ways that he had brought with him from St. Louis. On August 1, Lanier was listed as the top starting pitcher in the league with an .857 winning percentage and a 6–1 record in nine games. Had Lanier combined his victories with the Cards and his victories with the Blues he would have posted a 12-game winning streak before absorbing his first loss of the season. He was pitching as well as he ever had. Lanier had been in the 1942, 1943, and 1944 World Series for the Cardinals and had done well. In those three years he had won 13, 15, and 17 games for St. Louis during the regular season.

In August, the Blues had a four-game home series against the first-place Tampico Cotton Pickers. Tampico took three of the four games with their only loss coming in the game in which the lefty Lanier went to the mound. Lanier threw a three hitter and struck out 14 Cotton Pickers.

Max Lanier continued to rack up victories in Mexico in 1946 after beginning the season with the St. Louis Cardinals and recording a 6–0 record (National Baseball Hall of Fame Library, Cooperstown, N.Y.).

11 ◆ Lou Klein, Max Lanier, and Fred Martin

On August 6, Lanier was in St. Petersburg, Florida, undergoing treatment for his ailing elbow. He said that he was not going to leave the Mexican League as Owen had done, saying that he had been treated well by those connected with Pasquel's league. He had received a bonus, a handsome salary, and hotel accommodations as good as the New York hotel in which the Cardinals stayed on their trips to the "Big Apple."

Toward the end of the season, there was a rumor that Lanier was going to be shipped from the Vera Cruz club to the Mexico City team to help them in their fight for the pennant. Vera Cruz was hopelessly out of the race and since Jorge Pasquel owned both clubs he was considering taking the strength from one club to help the other. The fact that both teams called Mexico City "home" would have made the exchange quick and easy. However, fans all over Mexico protested the move, and Tampico, who was tied with the Reds at the time, said they wouldn't play their games if Lanier was moved to Mexico City. Pasquel decided against the "trade" because of the reaction against it. It certainly must have been one of the few times that Jorge Pasquel bowed to the will of the people.

Bernardo Pasquel traveled to Paris in September, and on his return he made a stopover in New York City. While he was there he announced that the Mexican League was considering inviting five of the top major leaguers to visit Mexico for a vacation after the World Series. He also said that he and his brothers would take the opportunity to have some conversations with them about joining their clubs for the 1947 season. He identified Ted Williams, Johnny Pesky, and Bob Feller as three of the five that he was talking about. While he was on the subject of the approaching World Series, he mentioned the National League's down-to-the-wire race between the Cardinals and the Dodgers, and he commented, saying, "Brooklyn should be grateful to the Mexican League for taking pitcher Max Lanier away from the Cards. Otherwise Brooklyn would be 10 games behind, rather than half a game."[4]

On September 23, it was reported by "league officials" that Lanier, Klein, and Harry Feldman, who had come to Mexico from the Giants, had abandoned the Blues after the three players failed to appear for Sunday's final game of a five-games road series against Tampico. The players all immediately denied the report and, when the situation was sorted out, it appeared that it had resulted from some confused communication.

Klein said that there had not been any trouble, as had been reported, between himself and manager Chile Gomez, who had taken over as the Vera Cruz manager after Owen's departure. He said he had a recurrent attack of appendicitis, and that he would be back on the field when the schedule resumed on Thursday. Feldman reported that both he and Lanier had sore arms and they had been given permission by Gomez to return home to rest.

It appeared that the root of the confusion was that Gomez had given the three players permission to miss the game, and that was something that only Jorge Pasquel, and not Gomez, was permitted to do.

It was also announced that another rumor did not have any truth to it. There had been a report that Lanier would pitch in all four of the games of the final series against Mexico City. Rueda Magro, a league official, said that was not possible because league rules would not allow it.

Vera Cruz's final game of the season was against Puebla at Delta Park. It was a rainy day, and many players on both sides probably were rooting for a rainout. Vera Cruz could avoid ending up in the basement by not playing. However, the rain stopped and the game was played, with the Blues winning by a sizeable margin. Before the game, Klein was amazed by the number of people who had come out to watch the meaningless game. The overflow crowd was allowed to stand in foul territory while the game was in progress.

Lanier was the starting pitcher, and he had been rushed to the mound after the rain stopped without having the time to properly warm up. With his continuing arm troubles, he usually took extra time to get ready to pitch. He was angry that he hadn't been given sufficient time to get his arm warm and loose. Puebla's four runs crossed the plate in the top of the first inning before the Blues recorded their first out and before Lanier was ready to pitch. Lanier worked himself into a groove, and the left-hander went six innings and left the game with a 11–4 lead.

The ex–Cardinal finished the season with an impressive 8–3 record, although he had suffered a bump in the road after beginning his Mexican League career by going 6–0 to match his season's start in St. Louis. He pitched 107 innings in 18 games for the Blues, throwing five complete games with one shutout. His ERA was a stingy 1.93, which was tops in the league.

The other two imports from St. Louis also had impressive seasons. Klein singled in the season finale and finished the campaign with a .335 batting average with 17 doubles. He appeared in 58 games for Vera Cruz.

Martin spent the season with Mexico City, which finished in second place behind Tampico. He appeared in 28 games for the Reds, going 12–6 with a 2.71 ERA.

Martin and Lanier remained in Mexico and played one more season. In 1947, Martin was with Mexico City for a second year where he appeared in 34 games with the Reds. He posted a 16–9 record with a 3.05 ERA.

That season, Lanier was back with Vera Cruz, but only pitched 46⅓ innings in 6 games and had a 2–2 record with a 1.17 ERA. Four of his outings were complete games, and he registered one shutout.

Klein was with the Monterrey Sultans in 1947, where he appeared in 79 games and batted .273 with 15 doubles for the league champions. He was not in the Mexican League in 1948, but he returned to Monterrey for another campaign in 1949. He only spent part of the season with Monterrey, which went on to capture its third consecutive championship. In 27 games, Klein hit .252 with 6 doubles. He would be back playing in 58 games for St. Louis after Chandler lifted the suspension before the end of the 1949 season.

♦ 12 ♦

Charlie Mead, Napoleon Reyes, and Adrian Zabala: The Pasquels Strike the Giants Again

Charlie Mead, Napoleon Reyes, and Adrian Zabala were three wartime players with the New York Giants. Each was born outside the United States and was not eligible for the military draft during World War II. Mead was born in Vermilion, Alberta, Canada, on April 9, 1921. Reyes and Zabala were born in Cuba. Reyes was born on November 24, 1919, in Santiago de Cuba, and Zabala was born on August 26, 1916, in San Antonio de Los Baños.

Mead made his major debut on August 28, 1943, and he appeared in 37 games that season, hitting .274 as a utility infielder for the Polo Grounders. He was in 39 games the following campaign and batted .179. In 1945, he saw action in only 11 games for the Giants and had a .270 batting average.

Reyes joined the Giants for his first major league game on May 19, 1943, in a 3–2 win over the Cincinnati Reds. Reyes was in 40 games during his rookie season, with 38 of them as a first baseman. He hit .256 during that stretch. The following campaign he split his play between first and third base, hitting an improved .289. In 1945, the 6'1", 205-pounder appeared in 122 of the Giants' games at third base. Reyes had 431 at bats and hit .289. He struck out only 26 times during the season. He had played regularly for two of his three seasons in the Polo Grounds before taking the Pasquels' money and running to their country.

Reyes was Danny Gardella's roommate on the road while he was with the Giants. Gardella was the only player on the club at the time who was willing to room with a Cuban. Reyes had been the object of Gardella's "suicide" joke when New York was in Cincinnati for a series in May, 1945.

Zabala debuted with the Giants on August 11, 1945, in St. Louis against the Cardinals. The left-handed pitcher, who had come from New York's minor league club in Jersey City, started five games in his first major league season and relieved in six others. He put together a 2–4 record with a 4.78 ERA.

Mead was not considered to be a "jumper" from Organized Baseball in the manner of most of the other players. The Giants had released the 25-year-old, 6'1½", 185-pound Canadian, in early April, 1946. With no place to play, he signed to join Vera Cruz on April 11. He went hitless as the starting right fielder in his first Mexican League game 10 days later. The Blues lost, 4–3, to the Monterrey Sultans.

Napoleon Reyes left the New York Giants in 1946 and began a lengthy career in the Mexican League (National Baseball Hall of Fame Library, Cooperstown, N.Y.).

Mead had a short-lived career in Mexico, appearing in only four games and going to bat 13 times. He had 3 hits for a .231 average.

Reyes, although he had performed well with New York in 1944 and 1945, did not see a bright future with the Giants in 1946. Rookie Bill Rigney appeared to be the third-base favorite.

Zabala was a holdout with the Giants during the pre–1946 campaign. He visited the club's spring training camp in Miami, Florida, on February 28, to meet with New York manager Mel Ott. The manager did not greet him with optimistic news. Ott told Zabala that his contract offer from the Giants was non-negotiable and that the pitcher's chances of making the Giants' regular season roster were slim. The manager informed him that a return to Jersey City was most likely.

Zabala left Miami and headed for Jacksonville, Florida, where the Jersey City club was training. His intent was not to join the minor leaguers but to visit friends there while he thought about Ott's words and mulled over a previous offer from the Pasquels, which he eventually decided to take.

Both Reyes and Zabala were assigned to the Puebla team. They were reunited with Adolfo Luque, the former Giants pitching coach and current manger of the Parrots. All three men were of Cuban heritage.

Reyes had one of the lengthier stays in the Mexican League of all of those who left the United States to play south of the border. He appeared in 93 games with Puebla in 1946, and he hit an outstanding .361. He had 20 doubles, 11 triples, six home runs, and 75 RBI. He finished only three percentage points behind Monterrey's Claro Duany, who won the league's batting championship.

The following two years he returned to be Puebla's third baseman. He hit .303 and .332 in 1947 and 1948 with Puebla. He was with Monterrey in 1949, his final season in the league. He was in 66 games and had a .270 batting average.

Zabala had been with Puebla in 1944 before he made his major league debut with the Giants a season later. He was 10–2 in his first season with the Mexican League team, with a league-leading 2.74 ERA. He made 18 appearances on the mound that summer. It appears as if most, if not all of them, would have been as a starter. That is not certain, however, because a record for starts by pitchers in the Mexican League was not kept until 1947.

When Zabala returned to Puebla for the 1946 season, he became one of the club's most regularly used hurlers. He appeared in 43 games and posted a 11–14 record with a 4.92 ERA. In 1947, his final year in the Mexican League, he was still with Puebla. With improved record keeping, we know that the left-hander made 34 starts among his 45 appearances during the season. Zabala posted a 19–14 record with a 3.40 ERA.

♦ 13 ♦

Ace Adams and Harry Feldman: Two Giants Pitchers Go to Mexico

On April 26, two New York Giant pitchers signed contracts to play in the Mexican League and left the club. The two right-handers — reliever Ace Adams and starter Harry Feldman — had signed $10,000 contracts and had received $10,000 bonuses to exchange their Giants uniforms for those of the Vera Cruz Blues. They became the seventh and eighth Giant players to accept offers from the Pasquels. Earlier in the spring, Adams had said that he had turned down a three-year, $80,000 offer to pitch south of the border. Jorge Pasquel was placing them with the Blues, one of the teams that he owned in the league, where they would join Danny Gardella, a former teammate in New York.

Manager Mel Ott reported that Adams and Feldman had come to the Polo Grounds to clean out their lockers while the Giants were doing their pre-game warmups before playing the first-place Brooklyn Dodgers.

Ott said, "I did not see either of them before they left. But I first noticed something was amiss when neither appeared on the field for pre-game practice. I went to the clubhouse to find out why they were absent, and Eddie Logan, our clubhouse man, told me they had been in, packed their stuff and departed."[1]

The Giants were 3–7 and sat in seventh place in the National League at the time of the two pitchers' departure.

Adams was born in Willows, California, on March 2, 1912. He

was purchased from the Nashville team after the 1940 campaign, and he made his major league debut with the Giants on April 15, 1941, in a relief appearance against the Dodgers that the Giants won, 6–4. Adams had a 4–1 record that season.

The 5'10½", 182-pounder was the Giants' durable bullpen ace during the war years. During the off-seasons Adams operated an expansive peanut plantation in Iron City, Georgia.

From the time of his debut in 1941 until his departure in 1946, Adams made 302 appearances on the mound for New York, only seven of them starter. He was 7–4 in 1942 with a 1.84 ERA in 61 games. In 1943, Adams went 11–7 with a 2.82 ERA in 70 appearances that totaled 140⅓ innings of work. The following season, he was in 65 games, with an 8–11 record and a 4.25 ERA in 137⅔ innings. In his final full season before leaving for Mexico, Adams was 11–9 with a 3.42 ERA in 65 games and 113 innings. He led the league with 13 saves in 1944 and with 15 in 1945.

Adams had signed his 1946 contract with the Giants on February 28. When he relieved Bill Voiselle on Opening Day at the Polo Grounds, it marked his 300th game with the Giants. He made two more appearances before leaving the team, and he posted a 0–1 record for the season and a 16.88 ERA.

Feldman was born in the Bronx on November 10, 1919. He joined the Giants' farm system in 1938, after he impressed Bill Terry, the club's manager, at a tryout camp. The right-hander went 13–1 as a rookie for Blytheville, Arkansas, in 1939.

After working his way up through the Giants' Jersey City club, he made his major league debut on September 10, 1941. In that game, the 6', 175-pounder lost, 10–7, to the Pittsburgh Pirates. On September 21, Feldman shut out the Boston Braves, 4–0. That day, Harry Danning was behind the plate, and he and Feldman might have formed the major leagues' first all–Jewish battery. He finished the season with a 1–1 record in three starts.

He was called to military service following the season, and he was found to be suffering from a tubercular condition. Following treatment, he was judged ready to resume his baseball career, but he wasn't going to be able to join the military.

13 ♦ Ace Adams and Harry Feldman

Pitcher Harry Feldman has his best season with the New York Giants in 1945. A year later he was with the Vera Cruz Blues of the Mexican League (National Baseball Hall of Fame Library, Cooperstown, N.Y.).

Mexican Raiders in the Major Leagues

In 1942, Feldman came out of the bullpen in 25 of his 31 appearances and finished the season with a 7–1 record and a 3.16 ERA. He was 4–5 in 1943, mainly as a reliever and them moved into the Giants' starting rotation the following season when he went 11–13 with a 4.16 ERA for the fifth-place Polo Grounders. He picked up the decision in the franchise's most lopsided victory with a 26–8 win over the Dodgers on April 30, 1944. In 1945, he had his best season with the Giants, going 12–13 with a 3.27 ERA. Thirty of his 35 appearances came in the role of a starter.

Before leaving the Giants for Mexico in 1946, Feldman struggled in three games and was 0–2 with a lofty 18.00 ERA.

Adams arrived in Mexico City on the last day of April. He was accompanied by Mexican League scout Robert Janis, and two of the Pasquel brothers, Alfonso and Gerardo. Shortly thereafter, Adams went on a brief vacation to Acapulco with Jorge Pasquel before joining the Vera Cruz team. He flew to Torreon on May 9 to meet up with the Blues for their weekend series there against the Alijadores (cotton ginners).

While Adams was in Torreon, Feldman, who had arrived in Mexico about a week after his Giant teammate, was working out in Mexico City and acclimating himself to the area's climate.

Feldman mentioned that he had spoken with Ott by telephone from his home in Ft. smith, Arkansas, before leaving the country.

On the day that Adams departed for Torreon, Feldman acknowledged that he had gotten quite tired running during his first workout south of the border. He wondered how the high altitude would affect his curveball. He was expected to join the team in the middle of the following week when the players returned from Torreon.

It was a long season for the two ex–Giant pitchers. The Vera Cruz team was struggling to stay out of the league's cellar even though they had, at one time or another, 11 players from Organized Baseball that Jorge Pasquel had hand-picked. He expected the Blues to be the class of the league, showing fans in the capital city what the future of the "new" Mexican League was going to be like in the years to come. Pasquel's dream was not to be realized in 1946.

Feldman did have an outstanding afternoon on May 30 in a game against the Puebla Parrots. He faced former fellow Giant Sal Maglie who was on the mound for the Parrots. The two hurlers hooked up in an 11-inning scoreless tie that was finally halted because of rain. Each pitcher surrendered only five hits. The matchup was one of the Mexican League's best pitching duels in years.

Adams made 32 appearances for the Blues, all in relief. He pitched 134⅓ innings and finished with a 5–7 record and a 4.02 ERA for the lowly Vera Cruz team. Feldman made 33 starts for the Blues and pitched 161⅓ innings. He had a 5–15 record with a 3.79 ERA.

Unlike some of the others who left the major leagues and spent more than the 1946 season south of the border, Adams and Feldman were one-season players in the Mexican League. Like Jorge Pasquel, these two pitchers had not found the 1946 season in Mexico to be the successful experience they had hoped it would be.

However, they might not have found any more happiness with the Giants. The season wasn't going well back in New York for Adams' and Feldman's former club. The Giants finished in the basement of the National League, posting a dismal 61–93 record. The Polo Grounders ended the season 36 games behind the pennant-winning and World Series champion St. Louis Cardinals.

◆ 14 ◆

Alex Carrasquel and Roberto Ortiz: Two Washington Senators Find a Place in Mexico

Alex Carrasquel and Roberto Ortiz, two players with ties to the Washington Senators, were among the group of 23 major leaguers who went to Mexico to play baseball in that country's top league. Both players were part of Senators president Clark Griffith's plan to bring Latin American players to strengthen the Washington club. Carrasquel was the first Venezuelan to play in the major leagues, and Ortiz followed him to Washington. Bobby Estalella and Rene Monteaugudo, who also went to Mexico, were other Latin Americans to join the Senators during that time.

Carrasquel was born on July 24, 1912, in Caracas, Venezuela. He made his major league debut on April 23, 1939, in a one-inning relief appearance in a 7–4 loss to the New York Yankees. The right-hander possessed an effective fastball, a dancing knuckleball, and a decent curveball. His debut was an impressive and promising outing in which he retired the Yankees in order. He struck out Joe DiMaggio, got a ground ball out on Lou Gehrig, and registered a pop out on Bill Dickey.

Most of the 255 games he appeared in with the Senators from 1939 through 1945 were as a reliever. He won 50 games and lost 39 during that span. His best record was in 1943 when he went 11–7 with a 3.68 ERA. He posted his lowest ERA in 1945 with 2.71 and had a 7–5 record.

Carrasquel was purchased by the Chicago White Sox from the Senators on January 2, 1946. The right-hander signed a three-year contract to play in the Mexican League on February 28, 1946, after weighing the option of going south or remaining in Chicago. Chicago general manager Leslie M. O'Connor claimed to be shocked when the club's recent acquisition, who he said had committed to play for the White Sox, joined the Vera Cruz Blues.

Roberto Ortiz, who was born in Camaguey, Cuba, on June 30, 1915, made his major league debut with the Senators on September 6, 1941. The outfielder appeared in 22 games late in that season, and he hit .329 in 79 at bats. During the remainder of his time in Washington, he was a reserve for the Senators, never quite making it as a front-line player, even during the wartime years.

He was in only 20 games in 1942, making 42 plate appearances and struggling with a .167 bating average. The following season, Ortiz appeared in only one game and picked up one hit in his four at-bats. In 1944, he was used in 85 games, hit .253 with five home runs and 35 RBI. He took an offer from the Mexican League for the 1945 campaign. In so doing, he began to display skills that he had not yet shown in Organized Baseball.

Ortiz, a center fielder, was the Mexican League's home run champion in 1945. He appeared in 86 games with the Mexico City Reds and had a .336 batting average, hit 24 doubles, and drove in 92 runs. Ortiz's 26 home runs was tops in the league. The number of home runs that he hit was one thing; the distances they traveled was often something else. What would have been a 350-foot blast in the United States sometimes turned into a 500-foot shot in the higher elevations. Several of Ortiz's 26 round-trippers were of that variety.

Ortiz was back with Mexico City for the opening game of the 1946 season. He banged his first home run of the year in the Reds' 12–5 loss to Vera Cruz.

The Blues dropped the second game of the season to the Reds, 10–6. Ortiz homered again, and his second blast of the campaign was off Carrasquel, the Vera Cruz starter. The Blues' hurler struggled early, and it appeared that manager Ramon Bragana wanted to remove Carrasquel early in the game, but a few words with Jorge Pasquel, as he was heading to the mound to make the move, changed his mind. The Reds' lead reached 7–0 before Bragana took Carrasquel out of the game. Bragana was at the Blues' helm for the first part of the season before Mickey Owen assumed the position.

Carrasquel was on the mound the following day for the third game in the opening series with the Reds. He struggled again, and didn't make it out of the first inning, surrendering five singles and three doubles to the Reds' hitters. His record already stood at 0–2.

On April 16, Carrasquel spoke about the conditions there and appeared to be happy about being in Mexico. Others were experiencing some problems with the living and playing conditions, but he was not among them. Carrasquel had missed Opening Day in Organized Baseball, and said, "I have no regrets — who would, leaving the White Sox?"[1]

The right-hander made regular appearances on the mound for the Blues early in the campaign, both as a starter and as a reliever. On April 25, he went the distance for a 7–3 win against Torreon. He scattered 11 hits, giving up the three runs in the third inning. Two former players from Organized Baseball helped to produce the runs. Carrasquel issued a base on balls that was followed by a single to former New York Giant George Hausmann, and then a three-run homer to former Philadelphia Phillies pitcher-outfielder Rene Monteaugudo.

However, about a month later, there was a newspaper report that the 32-year-old Vera Cruz pitcher had been released by Jorge Pasquel. The report was denied by Carrasquel, who had relieved Harry Feldman in the eighth inning of a losing game against Torreon the previous day. Carrasquel was upset after he was rushed into the game with Torreon holding a sizable lead. That was his twelfth appearance of the season and his record stood at 4–4.

The White Sox quickly issued a statement that they didn't want Carrasquel back with them if he left Mexico. There had been an earlier report that the pitcher had telephoned the White Sox with the hope that he might be able to return and play for them in Chicago. White Sox road secretary Frank McMahon said that the telephone call was news to him and that no one with the team was paying any attention to him.

The incident between Pasquel, Carrasquel, and the Blues was cleared up on May 18. The pitcher explained that it was the result of an argument that he had with Bragana. The argument followed Bragana's use of Carrasquel in the game against Torreon. He told Bragana that the manager's move was foolish and that he wanted to be moved to the Mexico City club. Jorge Pasquel's initial reaction had been to say that he wanted to get rid of the pitcher altogether. The issue was resolved, and Carrasquel remained with the Blues, at least for the time being.

Carrasquel did end up with Mexico City before the end of the season, but it wasn't because of Bragana. Jorge Pasquel reassigned him to the Reds after Owen became the Vera Cruz manager.

Owen had not played with African Americans on his former teams, and he didn't want to have to catch them in the Mexican League. Carrasquel, a Venezuelan, was not black but he was close enough for Owen. Owen made his feelings known to Jorge Pasquel, and he moved Carrasquel to the Reds. Vera Cruz was becoming known as the "Whites" rather than the "Blues" as a result of a number of similar moves that purged the team of those players who were black or were close to it.

Ortiz had a good offensive start to the season but he didn't enjoy some of the changes that had occurred with the influx of new players. For him, the atmosphere improved as the season progressed and baseball was being played the way he liked it.

On August 1, Ortiz was at the top of the league again in the home-run race. He had hit 16 homers in 257 times at bat. Estalella trailed him with 14 round trippers.

During most of the season, Tampico, Mexico City, and Monterrey waged a close three-team race in the Mexican League. In the end, Tampico finished at the top of the league with the Reds in the second spot. Monterrey fell out of contention and finished in fifth place.

Ortiz hit .332 while playing in 99 games in 1946, his second season in the league. Once again he led the loop in round-trippers, slamming 25. He also added 28 doubles, 13 triples, and a league-high 108 RBI to his offensive output.

Unlike others who had come from Organized Baseball to take the Pasquel's money and then run back to the Unites States or elsewhere,

Ortiz became a fixture south of the border. He was with the Reds again in 1947, hitting .307, driving in 82 runs, and leading the league in homers for the third consecutive year with 22. He was back at it in 1948, leading the Reds and the league in both homers and RBI. He had 19 home runs and 74 runs-batted-in.

Ortiz left the league for the next three seasons but returned to play there again in 1952, 1955, and 1956. He was named to the Mexican League Hall of Fame in 1973.

Despite his early disagreements and discomfort in 1946, Carrasquel also had a lengthy Mexican League career. In 1946, during the influx of players from Organized Baseball, he had a 13–8 record in 36 games with a 4.50 ERA with Vera Cruz and Mexico City.

He divided the 1947 season between Mexico City and Monterrey, going a combined 13–11 with a 3.03 ERA. Carrasquel was back with Monterrey the following campaign and was 18–8 with a 3.18 earned-run-average. He appeared in 41 games, making 25 starts and tossing 17 complete games. He had a short season with Torreon in 1949 before returning to Organized Baseball for a brief stay with the White Sox. Carrasquel's name would reappear in Mexican League boxscores in 1952, 1954, 1955, and 1956. He had a 53–36 career won-loss record in the Mexican League with a 3.60 ERA.

♦ 15 ♦

Bobby Estalella, Myron Hayworth, and Rene Monteagudo: Three Pasquel Pickups

Roberto "Bobby" Estalella, Myron "Red" Hayworth, and Rene Monteagudo went to Mexico for the 1946 season and remained there for the following season. Nothing was available to them in Organized Baseball in 1947 because of commissioner A.B. "Happy" Chandler's five-year suspension of those who had gone south of the border.

Estalella was born in Cardenas, Cuba, on April 25, 1911. He made his major league debut with the Washington Senators on September 7, 1935, and hit .314 in 15 games that season. He was part of Senators president Clark Griffith's harvest of Latin American players.

The following season, the outfielder was in only 13 games, and he did not appear in a major league lineup again until 1939 when he was in 82 games, batting .275 with eight home runs and 41 RBI. He left Washington for the 1941 season, and played for the St. Louis Browns in 46 games that year.

Wartime baseball gave him the opportunity to play more regularly at the major league level. As a draft-exempt player because he was born in Cuba, Estalella was back with Washington in 1942, and he played in 133 games, splitting his time between the outfield and third base. He was traded to the Philadelphia Athletics for 1943. He posted a .259 batting average in 117 games. He had 11 home runs and 63 RBI.

In 1944, the 5'8", 180-pound, right-handed hitter was a regular

Mexican Raiders in the Major Leagues

outfielder for Philadelphia, appearing in 144 games, the most of his major league career. He hit .298, which was the best of his career as a regular on a major league team. He followed that with a .299 batting average for the Athletics in 1945. He also had a very respectable .435 slugging percentage.

Hayworth, a catcher, was born in High Point, North Carolina, on May 14, 1915. He was the younger brother of Ray Hayworth, also a catcher, who played 15 seasons in the majors, beginning in 1926 and ending in 1945, mostly with the Detroit Tigers. "Red" Hayworth struggled with injuries throughout his time in the minors. His best season was in 1943, when he displayed his strong throwing arm and hit .278 for Toledo. He made his major league debut with the Browns on April 21, 1944. Although Hayworth only hit .222 in his first season in St. Louis, he played an important role in working with the pitching staff. He shared the catching duties with Frank Mancuso. Hayworth started all six games of the 1944 World Series, which the Browns lost to the St. Louis Cardinals, 4 games to 2. He hit .118 in that season's Fall Classic.

The following year, Hayworth was in only 56 games and batted .194. Regardless of this anemic offensive output, he was on the Pasquels' list of players to bring to Mexico.

The younger Hayworth brother remembered when his older sibling returned from playing the 1930 season with the Tigers. It had been the first summer of his lengthy career when he had been an integral part of his team. Ray had driven home to High Point that fall in his new sleek black Cadillac. That soon became part of the goals of the then 15-year-old "Red." However, the Cadillac appeared to be far from a reality, the way his career was progressing. Also at that time, because of the war, there was a long waiting list for new Cadillacs.

"Red" first met with Bernardo Pasquel two days before the opening of the 1946 major league season. Although he would make at least twice the salary in Mexico that he had signed for with the Browns, Hayworth was having difficulty with the idea of leaving Organized Baseball. Teammate Vern Stephens' brief negative experience in Mexico added to Hayworth's concerns. The possibility of being suspended by Commissioner A.B. Chandler also was on his mind.

15 ♦ Bobby Estalella, Myron Hayworth, and Rene Monteagudo

Pasquel continued to urge Hayworth to take the opportunity south of the border. According to one account, it was that dream of owning a Cadillac that was the final determiner.

After a meeting in St. Louis with Bernardo Pasquel in which Hayworth was still unable to give him a positive response to the plan to have the catcher go to Mexico, the two men exited the hotel where the meeting had taken place. Outside the hotel, Hayworth was given the keys to a brand-new black Cadillac. That sealed the deal. He had made his decision to go south of the border.

Hayworth soon was off to Mexico. He suited up in a Torreon uniform and played with the club in 1946. He had arrived in Mexico a couple of weeks after the start of the season, and he took the position that Jorge Pasquel originally had promised to Mickey Owen. Owen never made it to Torreon and was behind the plate in Vera Cruz.

A couple of days after arriving in Mexico and hearing that Chandler's plan for the suspensions had gone into effect, Hayworth said that he was "perfectly happy" in his new working environment.[1]

Monteagudo was born on March 12, 1916, in Havana, Cuba. The 5'7", 165-pound left-hander made his debut with the Senators on September 6, 1938. He was another of Griffith's Latin American imports, and he offered something that none of the other 23 "jumpers" offered. He was both an outfielder and a pitcher.

All of Monteagudo's appearances during his initial season with the Senators were as a pitcher. He was in five games, three as a starter. He worked 22 innings and had a 1–1 record with a 5.73 ERA. In 1940 with Washington he was 2–6 with a 6.08 ERA. He started eight of the 27 games in which he appeared. In 1944 with Washington he hit .289 in 10 games as an outfielder. He did not pitch for Washington that season.

Monteagudo was with the Phillies in 1945, primarily as an outfielder, but he was also in 14 games as a relief pitcher. He hit .301 and had a 0–0 record on the mound with a 7.49 ERA.

Estalella reported to the Vera Cruz Blues when he arrived in the Mexican League. Later in the season, the outfielder was sent to San Luis Potosi. The 5'8", 180-pound, right-handed slugger was known as "Tarzan" to his fans in the league. On August 1, Estallela was trailing

Roberto Ortiz, his former Senator teammate, in the home run race, 16–14. He appeared in 97 games in 1946, hitting 21 home runs and sporting a .306 batting average with 66 RBI.

He remained with San Luis Potosi in 1947, his final Mexican League season. He hit .285 in 122 games and legged out 29 doubles. His home run output dropped to eight, but he increased his RBI total to 82.

Hayworth also played two seasons south of the border. With Torreon in 1946, Hayworth finished with a .261 average in 81 games. The catcher had 17 doubles and drove in 47 runs. The following season, he joined Estalella with San Luis Potosi. He hit .270 in 70 games.

Monteagudo was primarily an outfielder during a four-year Mexican League career, but he did make an occasional appearance as a relief pitcher. In 1946, he was with Torreon, batting .339 in 97 games. He hit 27 doubles and drove in 78 runs. He made two appearances in relief and was 0–0 with a 5.59 ERA.

He spent time with both Vera Cruz and San Luis Potosi in 1947. He repeated his output of 78 RBI with a .326 batting average in 122 games. He went to the mound in three games, two of them as a starting pitcher, putting together a 0–1 record with a 8.44 ERA. Monteagudo began the 1948 campaign with San Luis Potosi and was back with Vera Cruz before the season's end. He was in the outfield in 86 games, hitting a lofty .366. His pitching was limited to 1/3 of an inning of relief.

Monteagudo played his final Mexican League season in 1949, playing for San Luis Potosi and then joining the Mexico City Reds. He did not appear on the mound that summer. He was in the outfield for 77 games and hit .310.

◆ 16 ◆

Moe Franklin, Roland Gladu, and James Steiner: They Saw Brighter Futures in Mexico

The final three players in the group of 23 "jumpers" to the Mexican League were peripheral to their major league teams. They never caught on with clubs in the United States and were easily expendable for the 1946 season.

Murray "Moe" Franklin was born in Chicago, Illinois, on April 1, 1914. He led Organized Baseball in batting in 1938 when he hit a gaudy .439 for Beckley, West Virginia, the Detroit Tigers' minor league club in the Mountain States League. Although he won *The Sporting News'* Louisville Slugger Award as the player with the highest average in all of baseball, the accomplishment was not impressive enough for Detroit to bring him to the majors. He finally made his major league debut with the Tigers on August 12, 1941. The infielder hit .300 in 13 games. Franklin was back with Detroit in 1942, and he batted .260 in 48 games.

Franklin then served in the U.S. Navy, and returned to civilian life in 1945. He was not wanted by the Tigers after his return, and his hopes and dreams for a baseball career turned to Mexico.

He spent two seasons in Mexico. He was the shortstop with league champion Tampico in 1946, where he hit .300 in 85 games. Franklin was back with Tampico in 1947, appearing in 46 games and hitting .213.

Not much is known about the professional career of Roland Edouard Gladu. The records are available for his two years in the

Mexican League (1946 and 1947), but not much is known about the details of his life and accomplishments during those two seasons.

Gladu was born on May 10, 1911, in Montreal, Quebec, Canada, and he made his major league debut with the Boston Braves on April 18, 1944. He was in 21 games with the Braves that season. He played three games in the outfield, 15 games at third base, and pinch-hit in three others, hitting .242.

In 1945, the French-Canadian infielder was with the Dodgers' top minor league club in Montreal where he led to club in batting. He played winter ball in Havana after the season. On February 28, 1946, Gladu announced that he had signed a three-year, $25,000 contract to play in the Mexican League.

In 1946, he was with Nuevo Laredo. He played in 91 games and had a good year at the plate, hitting .322. He had 17 doubles, 11 triples, and four home runs with 62 RBI. The following season he was with San Luis Potosi where he also hit .322 in 115 games. He had 27 doubles, a pair of triples, six home runs, drove in 79 runs, and then headed back to Canada, where he hit over .300 for four straight seasons in the Provincial League.

Harry "Red" Steiner was born in Los Angeles, California, on January 7, 1915. He made his major league debut on May 11, 1945, with the Cleveland Indians. The catcher played in only 12 games with the Indians that season before being sent to the Boston Red Sox, where he was in 26 games. He hit a combined .190 with the two clubs in 1945.

Steiner's hitting improved after he arrived in Mexico, where he played for Nuevo Laredo in 1946. He caught in 91 games for Nuevo Laredo and hit .306.

He was with Vera Cruz the following season and hit .295 while playing in 85 games for the Blues. Steiner was not in the Mexican League in 1948, and his final season in the loop was 1949 when he caught for Nuevo Laredo. He was behind the plate in 85 games, hitting .284.

♦ 17 ♦

The Mexican League in 1947 and Beyond

The 1946 season had been a disappointment for Jorge Pasquel and his brothers in many ways. They owned the Vera Cruz Blues, who had 11 jumpers in their lineup during the season, which was the largest number of imports from Organized Baseball. The Blues had been unable to compete with other teams in the league and finished in seventh place, one spot out of the cellar. Mexico City, the Pasquels' other team, had four players from major league baseball, and they ended the season in second place. Tampico, with Moe Franklin as the club's only import, captured the league's championship. The post-season playoffs were cancelled because of the financial problems that had battered the league.

Jorge Pasquel had tried to create a "major league team" and a Mexican Major League in the blink of an eye. He wanted it all to happen in the summer of 1946. When that didn't happen, Pasquel was disappointed and even he had a sense of failure. The "little boy" who loved the thrill of baseball, who was also one of Mexico's most powerful people, had a bit of his dreams destroyed that year.

Jorge and Bernardo Pasquel had to struggle to get the Mexican League going in 1947, although they had expressed renewed optimism earlier about the upcoming season. Jorge Pasquel had said at the league's winter meetings in mid–December, 1946, that he expected all of the players from Organized Baseball, with the exception of Mickey Owen and Alex Carrasquel, to return for the following season. Owen's departure appeared to be permanent, and Carrasquel, who had fought with

Mexican Raiders in the Major Leagues

the Pasquels throughout the season, did not leave Mexico in a happy mood or with positive feelings about Jorge Pasquel.

On a couple of occasions during the meetings, Jorge Pasquel intimated that he expected Ted Williams to come to Mexico in January. There was a plan in place for the teams to play 112 games in 1947. That meant that each team would play each other two more times than they had played in the previous season. The clubs had played 98 games in 1946.

As the new season approached, the Pasquels were met with resistant players and financial difficulties among some of the clubs.

Players who had not been imports in 1947 now wanted a fair share of the money. They were aware of the large salaries that had been given to the imports, many of whom had turned out not to be the top players on their clubs. Because of the league's financial difficulties, some of the imports had been notified that they would find sizable cuts in their contracts for the upcoming season.

Max Lanier was one of the resistant players. He had been asked to take a 50 percent cut from his 1946 salary because of the drain that the jumpers had put on the league's available money the previous summer. Following the conclusion of Cuba's winter season, many of those who had played in the Mexican League in 1946 staged a holdout there. The players who were demonstrating their dissatisfaction included many of those who had originally been in Organized Baseball, and others who had played almost exclusively in Mexico. There appeared to be four holdout groups in Cuba: the U.S. whites; the Cuban players; the U.S. Negroes; and the Mexicans. The total of the players in the four groups approached 120 players.

Jorge Pasquel spoke to the issue of finances and expressed an approach to the use of his funds that differed from what he had said during the previous season:

> The fact that I have much money has been mistakenly interpreted. There's no reason for giving it away, presenting exaggerated advances to players who instead of playing in accordance with their class come here, sit down with the money in their pockets, and either turn out failures or leave without thanks.[1]

17 ♦ The Mexican League in 1947 and Beyond

Jorge Pasquel did not want to risk a late start to the season, which tentatively was set for the middle of March, because it would cost him and the league a significant amount of income. He rejected his original plan to "hold out on the holdouts." On February 20, he headed for Havana, Cuba, to meet the rebellion. He met with the holdouts and was able, during several conversations, to settle a number of the issues with them. There were, however, a number in the group who were not yet ready to jump back to Mexico and resume their careers there. Lanier was among the still resistant players, and he did not report to play with the Blues until June 16.

Back in the United States, the New York Yankees and the New York Giants had headed back to court in November to seek a permanent injunction against the Mexican League's raids on players in Organized Baseball. Along with the Brooklyn Dodgers, they had been given a temporary injunction early in the 1946 season that barred the Mexican League from seeking to induce major league players to jump their signed contracts. Now, the owners of the two clubs sought to have the injunction take on a permanent status. The New York Supreme Court's decision on the request was postponed, and the prior temporary restraining order continued in effect.

Jorge Pasquel announced in March that he would not launch future raids on Organized Baseball. Mexican League owners and players received his assurance that the methods employed in 1946 to attract players would not be repeated for the 1947 season. Players who had not seen an increase in their incomes the previous season would no longer watch players come from the United States and immediately become the wealthiest members of their clubs. That was part of the message he had given to the holdout players during his meetings with them in Cuba.

Jorge Pasquel had announced that the league had basically broken even in 1946. However, many owners had felt financial distress during 1946, and they were not willing to see it repeated. The Blues, who played their home games at Delta Park in Mexico City, which had the largest seating capacity and had the largest fan base, lost the most money that season. San Luis Potosi, with the smallest playing field, also finished in the red. Not all of the clubs lost money. According to reports, Monterrey had a gross take that increased from $55,000 in 1945 to $120,000 in 1946.

It was announced that the eight-team league of the 1946 season would be reduced to six clubs in 1947. However, as was the case throughout the league, several scenarios appeared before the final set of six teams was in place.

Nuevo Laredo was the first team to withdraw for the 1947 campaign, and San Luis Potosi followed a short time later, leaving the six-team loop. Erasmo Flores, the president of the Nuevo Laredo club that had lost $12,000 during the 1946 season, said, "If Señor Pasquel doesn't mend his dictatorial ways soon, his league may fold up."[2]

Two days before the league's opening games on March 27, Angel Savaria, the president of the Torreon club, wired Jorge Pasquel to inform him that his team was not in any position to play in 1947. League officials made a quick decision to reinstate the San Luis Potosi team and return to six clubs. Torreon's players were transferred to San Luis Potosi.

The new schedule showed that each of the league's six teams (Mexico City, Monterrey, Puebla, San Luis Potosi, Vera Cruz, and Tampico) would play 120 games over a 30-week season. On opening day, the Blues beat the Mexico City Reds, 6–2, at Delta Park. An overflow crowd of 30,000 fans watched as 20-year-league veteran Ramon Bragana, one of Jorge Pasquel's favorite players, held the Reds to three hits.

The following "16 jumpers" (and the teams they were with in 1947 and future seasons) were back playing in the Mexican League. Contrary to Jorge Pasquel's earlier announcement, Carrasquel had returned. He had seven more seasons in the league ahead of him.

Alex Carrasquel	47 Mexico City, Monterrey; 48 Monterrey; 49 Torreon; 52 Monterrey; 54 Monterrey; 55 Tigres; 56 Mexico City
Bobby Estalella	47 San Luis Potosi
Moe Franklin	47 Tampico
Roland Gladu	47 San Luis Potosi
George Hausmann	47 Monterrey; 49 Nuevo Laredo

17 ♦ The Mexican League in 1947 and Beyond

Myron "Red" Hayworth	47 San Luis Potosi
Lou Klein	47 Monterrey; 49 Monterrey
Max Lanier	47 Vera Cruz
Sal Maglie	47 Puebla
Fred Martin	47 Mexico City
Rene Monteagudo	47 San Luis Potosi, Vera Cruz; 48 Vera Cruz
Luis Olmo	47 Vera Cruz
Roberto Ortiz	*45 Mexico City; 47 Mexico City; 48 Mexico City; 52 Nuevo Laredo; 55 Yucatan; 56 Yucatan
Napoleon Reyes	47 Puebla; 48 Puebla; 49 Mexico City
James Steiner	47 Vera Cruz; 49 Nuevo Laredo
Adrian Zabala	*44 Puebla; 47 Puebla

The following seven players who had spent time in the Mexican League in 1946 did not return after that season:

>Ace Adams
>Harry Feldman
>Danny Gardella
>Charlie Mead
>Mickey Owen
>Vern Stephens
>Roy Zimmerman

On October 28, 1947, baseball commissioner A.B. Chandler reiterated his position that the five-year suspension for players who left Organized Baseball for Mexico was still in place. Chandler's statement followed the announcement that the Mexican League had limited the number of non-Mexican players and their salaries in addition to promising not to have any more raids on the clubs in Organized Baseball.

With a large number of the six teams in the Mexican League losing money in 1947, the loop was reorganized, with Jorge Pasquel resigning as league president and Alejandro Aguilar Reyes succeeding him as commissioner in a new organizational structure.

Mexican Raiders in the Major Leagues

There was a flurry of activity between Organized Baseball and the Mexican League the following January that led some to believe that peace was on the horizon and that it might lead the commissioner to drop the five-year ban. Chandler sent Baseball Secretary Walter Mulbry to Mexico City to meet with Reyes.

After the meetings, Reyes announced that:

> all differences between the Mexican League and organized baseball in the United States have ended....
> Mr. Mulbry told me that Commissioner Chandler is greatly interested in reaching an agreement respecting the sovereignty of Mexican Baseball.[3]

There was some thought that the restructured Mexican League might even apply to join the National Association of Baseball Leagues (minor leagues).

The 31-year-old Mickey Owen, upon hearing the news of a possible reinstatement for the players, said, "I'll just sit tight and hope that nothing happens to keep me from being reinstated now.... I think I have several good years of baseball left because I have kept in shape."[4] Other suspended players expressed hope that their time in exile was nearly over.

The winds of optimism didn't blow long. Jorge Pasquel was back in the fray a few days later, announcing that he was out to try to interest more players from Organized Baseball to come to play in the Mexican League, and that Reyes' statements were not worth anything. Pasquel's statement prompted Reyes to resign as the league's commissioner. Reyes said, "If Pasquel wants to be the boss of the league, he can be the boss and have the league for all the foolishness he wants to do with it ... and I will bow out and go my own way."[5]

In 1947, the six-team league struggled, but made it through the season and into the 1948 campaign. In July of that year, two of the six teams dropped out of action, leaving only four clubs to finish the season that ended on September 19, a month before it was scheduled to conclude. Jorge Pasquel handed in his resignation as league president, and a new group of officers set out to build the league back to eight clubs, as it had operated in 1946. Matamoros and Guadalajara applied for membership in the new league.

17 ♦ The Mexican League in 1947 and Beyond

Owen and Jorge Pasquel continued their own battles through the seasons following 1946. Owen was preparing to fight the $127,500 suit that had been filed against him in Federal Court in Springfield, Missouri. In December 1946, it was announced that a group of established and quality baseball players would be called as witnesses during the hearing in the damage suit against Owen.

A month later, Owen hit Jorge Pasquel with a countersuit for breach of contract in U. S. District Court in Springfield. Owen's suit asked for $93,908.56 from Pasquel, who, he said, had removed him from his job as Vera Cruz's manager about July 5 and had failed to fulfill other promises. He asked for the return of $600 paid for personal expenses; $1,000 in house rent; a $51,428.56 difference between the amount of salary promised and the amount paid; and $40,880, which would be the amount of income tax he would owe in the United States.

Pasquel's suit against Owen and Owen's countersuit against Pasquel were heard in Federal Court in Springfield in 1949. When asked by Victor B. Harris, Jorge Pasquel's attorney, why he had not contacted Pasquel before he left Mexico, Owen said, "No need to see a man who fired you and doesn't have enough nerve to come up to your face and say: 'I don't need your services any more.'"[6]

One of Pasquel's charges against Owen was that he had difficulties with his teammates, especially blacks and Cubans. Owen denied the charge and, in his defense, said that he had had only one fight during his time in Mexico. That altercation was with Claro Duany, a Cuban outfielder who had slid into Owen at home plate while attempting to score. Owen described the situation, stating:

> He swung at me and I swung at him. The umpire jumped in and stopped it.
>
> That was the only trouble, even the only harsh words, I ever had in Mexico at any time — with players of any nationality or race.[7]

On April 7, 1949, former Giants pitcher Harry Feldman, Owen's Vera Cruz teammate, testified on behalf of Owen. He described for the jurors how Owen had been discharged by Jorge Pasquel, speaking about a paper which had been taken to the field by one of Pasquel's secretaries:

It was written in both Spanish and English, over Jorge Pasquel's signature. The paper stated that Owen had been relieved as manager of the club and replaced by a man named Gomez. The players were asked to sign paper, but Feldman never saw it again after he had affixed his signature.[8]

Shortly after Feldman's appearance, the case went to the jury of 10 men and two women. After two hours of deliberation by the jury, Pasquel's claims were turned town, and Owen was awarded $51,428.56 in damages. The amount awarded to Owen represented the unpaid portion of his salary for 1946 along with his complete salaries for 1947, 1948, and 1949.

In a follow-up to the court decision, the Springfield, Missouri, Chamber of Commerce authorized a request to Chandler for Owen's reinstatement in Organized Baseball. In the letter to Chandler, it was said that:

> He came back, admitted his error, and advised others not to go. Every baseball owner owes a debt of gratitude to Mickey Owen, because his action precluded the possibility of dozens of others trying to play south of he border.[9]

Pasquel asked for a new trial after the court granted Owen the money and turned down his own suit. Harris, Pasquel's lawyer, charged the judge with 14 errors in handling the case. On December 29, 1949, the United States Circuit Court of Appeals in St. Louis, in a unanimous decision, ruled that Owen was not entitled to the judgment that had been awarded against Jorge Pasquel.

The major element on which the decision was made centered on the title of Owen being a " player-manager." The Court of Appeals' ruling said the title was a misnomer, and the judge had erred in informing the jury that Owen was such. It was reported that:

> (Chief) Judge (Archibald K.) Gardner observed that Owen served as a player for the Vera Cruz team for six weeks before he managed the team for five. And then, after he was fired, stuck around as a player for six more.[10]

17 ♦ *The Mexican League in 1947 and Beyond*

Owen's case against Jorge Pasquel continued until 1952, when, on January 29, a Federal jury in Springfield, Missouri, returned a verdict for $35,000 in favor of Pasquel in his breach of contract suit against the former Vera Cruz Blues player. The basis for the verdict against Owen was that he had stayed on for a few days as a player after Pasquel had dismissed him as the team's manager. In doing so, he had waived his right to charge Pasquel with breach of contract.

At the time of the verdict, Owen was serving as catcher-coach for the Kansas City Blues of the American Association. Perhaps, he was the player who had lost the most as a result of his 1946 Mexican adventure.

◆ 18 ◆

Two More Suits

When the five-year suspension that had been instituted by baseball commissioner A.B. "Happy" Chandler continued beyond the 1946 season, there were two other suits filed. They were not against Jorge Pasquel and the Mexican League; they took dead aim at Organized Baseball.

Danny Gardella was the first to go to court, seeking redress for being suspended from baseball. On October 3, 1947, a suit was filed in federal court in New York City in which Gardella was seeking $300,000 in treble damages, claiming that his suspension had deprived him of a livelihood. Some of the defendants named in the suit were commissioner Chandler, National League president Ford C. Frick, American League president William Harridge, president of the minor leagues George M. Trautman, and the National Exhibition Company, who owned the New York Giants.

Later, Max Lanier and Fred Martin filed a suit against Organized Baseball for a combined $2,500,000.

Gardella's lawyer was Frederic A. Johnson, an attorney who knew both the law and baseball. Because Gardella had not signed a contract with the Giants for the 1946 season before leaving for Mexico, Johnson believed that his client had a legitimate case. In the affidavit, Johnson challenged the legality of the reserve clause. He also introduced a novel dimension, arguing that the presence of radio and television had extended the game into interstate commerce.

Organized Baseball filed a motion to dismiss the suit in New York District Court. On July 14, 1948, Judge Henry W. Goddard took the action, citing United States Supreme Court Justice Oliver Wendell

Mexican Raiders in the Major Leagues

Holmes' seminal ruling in 1922 in the case involving the Federal Baseball Club of Baltimore v. the National League of Professional Baseball Clubs.

Goddard said that he felt that he was bound in this case by the Supreme Court ruling that held that the leagues were not engaged in interstate commerce within the meaning of the Sherman Anti-Trust Act.

Gardella appealed the decision, and the case involving Gardella was heard first by the United States Court of Appeals for the Second Circuit. The three-man appellate court heard Johnson's argument and, on February 9, 1949, issued a 2–1 ruling in Gardella's favor. It was the opinion of the majority of the judges that the case was strong enough to merit a trial. The case was then sent back to District Court and a new trial was ordered on Gardella's contentions.

Judge Jerome N. Frank made it clear in the appeals decision that he thought the reserve clause of the standard baseball contract was illegal. He said that the Federal League decision:

> should be deemed to hold no more than that traveling of teams and their paraphernalia between states does not give rise to interstate commerce for Sherman Act purposes.[1]

In his opinion, Frank also questioned whether or not the televising and radio broadcasting of games brought Organized Baseball within the scope of anti-trust laws and whether it had violated those laws. If baseball was now within the scope of anti-trust laws, Holmes' ruling might no longer be relevant. The Court of Appeals directed the Federal District Court to determine whether, in fact, television and radio broadcasting had brought Organized Baseball within the scope of anti-trust laws and whether it had violated those laws.

Gardella, who was working at the time as an orderly for $36 a week in New York City's Mount Vernon Hospital, had scored a victory. He believed that rather than undermining baseball he was working to free players from the bondage created by the owners.

Horace Stoneham, the president of the Giants, said that he was happy with the judgment. He added, "The decision gives the case the right to go to trial. This is just what we want, since the case now will be thrown wide open."[2]

Chandler bristled at Frank's allegation that the reserve clause creates something resembling "peonage"— a term which, interestingly, Jorge Pasquel had used when he was encouraging players to leave Organized Baseball. The commissioner said, "no major leaguer makes less than $5,000 a year and some make up to $100,000.... If you call that peonage, then a lot of us would like to be in it."³

Once again, the era of the Mexican Raiders was causing the world of Organized Baseball some fear and frustration. In the opinion of some, "Gardella in the courtroom" was potentially more damaging than "Gardella in Mexico" had been.

The New York Giants' Horace Stoneham welcomed the court's intervention in the Gardella case (© S.F. Giants Archives).

Arthur Daley, writing in the *New York Times*, described Gardella's presence in both circumstances:

> Danny Gardella was a muscular midget who patrolled the outfield in his own inimitable tanglefoot style for the New York Giants. He was an amiable clown off the field and a less amiable clown on it. As a ballplayer he had no chance of breaking into the all-time outfield of Ruth, Cobb and Speaker. It is doubted that he could have broken past an outfield of Hart, Schaffner and Marx. Color he had. Talent he didn't have.⁴

Daley went on suggest that Gardella might become a quite memorable and important figure in baseball, taking a place alongside Abner Doubleday:

> It was Doubleday who is accorded the distinction of inventing our great American game. Dauntless Dan could very well become

> the fellow who destroyed it.... A judicial ruling that the reserve clause is illegal would be a body blow from which the sport could not recover.[5]

An indication of how seriously the ruling was being taken was seen in the responses from places as distant from each other as the Halls of Congress to the living rooms of retired ballplayers.

In the event that the trial's verdict went against Organized Baseball, certain members of Congress were attempting to pass legislation that would legalize the reserve clause and grant baseball an exception from antitrust laws. Arkansas congressman Wilbur Mills introduced such a bill in the House of Representatives. Representative A.S. (Syd) Herlong, a Florida Democrat and former president of the Florida State League, urged Gardella to reconsider his legal approach. Commenting about Gardella's trip to Mexico, Herlong said, "I sincerely hope that any player who would destroy baseball for personal gain, will for the sake of American youth, reconsider his action before it is too late."[6]

Several active and retired players were polled about their feeling regarding the reserve clause. Their responses indicated a general support of the clause under which they were playing or had played. Bob Dillinger of the St. Louis Browns responded by saying, "Everybody likes to be free. But it would cause a lot of confusion. So until something better is adopted, the rule should stay as is."[7] Stan Musial, who had been "courted" in 1946 by the Pasquels, commented, "I don't know much about the case, but I think baseball has done all right for 100 years the way it is."[8]

Mickey Owen, along with several of the other jumpers who had appealed to Organized Baseball for reinstatement, was not pleased with Gardella's legal fight. On the day following the Court of Appeals' decision, Owen reacted strongly:

> I hope Danny Gardella loses his suit against baseball....
> Baseball didn't force us to go to Mexico; we went because of our own weakness. Baseball needs the reserve clause, and while I am in the same boat as Gardella, I would not file suit to try to break it.[9]

18 ♦ Two More Suits

The month of March was a busy time for Organized Baseball and the courts. New York attorney John L. Flynn announced that a number of the players who had gone to Mexico to play baseball in 1946 would be following Gardella into the courtroom. He mentioned Max Lanier, Fred Martin, Lou Klein, Luis Olmo, Sal Maglie, Harry Feldman, Ace Adams, Myron Hayworth, and others as the players who would seek a final settlement for having been banned from Organized Baseball. When the final list appeared, Lanier and Martin were the only two players who were ready to file a suit. Perhaps others would follow later. It was announced originally that their suit would ask for more than $5,000,000 in damages. It turned out to be half that amount.

On March 8, Federal Judge John W. Clancy signed an order that directed Organized Baseball to show cause why it should not be restrained from prohibiting Lanier and Martin, both 33 years old, from playing baseball in the major leagues and from demanding that they sign contracts that contained a reserve or a termination clause. On March 11, the 16 major league clubs were served papers by United States Marshals. The papers required the clubs to answer a show cause order in New York as to why Martin and Lanier should not be allowed to play baseball in the major leagues.

On March 10, Johnson, Gardella's lawyer, announced that he was planning to go to Federal Court to ask for an injunction that would enable his client to be reinstated in Organized Baseball and be permitted to play immediately while awaiting the decision on his earlier appeal. The new action was a follow-up to what Lanier and Martin were seeking through the courts. Johnson, however, made it clear that he saw a major difference in the two suits, in that Lanier and Martin had jumped their 1946 signed contracts with the St. Louis Cardinals while Gardella was being held by the reserve clause because he had not signed a 1946 contract with the Giants.

Active players were beginning to make their opinions known about the suits, with special focus on the reserve clause. The Cardinals' player representative, Marty Marion, said that the Cards favored the establishment of a three-man arbitration panel to serve as an objective decision-maker in salary disputes. Several National League clubs had called meetings to vote on the reserve clause. Members of the Pittsburgh Pirates voted unanimously in support of that element of the Player Contract. There had been isolated player sentiment to retain the reserve clause, and the Pirates' vote was pleasing for Organized Baseball officials.

Organized Baseball was ordered by Federal Judge Edward A. Conger to show cause in court on March 15 why Gardella should not be reinstated. A two-hour hearing on the matter in New York City failed to resolve the issue, and the hearing was adjourned for a week. That hearing was later delayed until April 6. A new issue had been raised, and it was one on which the two sides differed. It questioned whether or not Chandler's suspension also prohibited Gardella, directly or indirectly, from playing amateur or semi-professional baseball.

On March 15, in Phoenix, Arizona, a similar hearing was held on the suit filed by Lanier and Martin, but it also failed to produce any decision about the reinstatements. That case was extended until April 29.

On March 23, Flynn made a motion that Maglie, another ex–Giant, join Lanier and Martin as a third plaintiff in their suit. Maglie, who was working as a gas station attendant in Lockport, New York, was seeking $1,000,000 in damages. Flynn announced later that he would withdraw the motion because of a technicality raised by the judge, and that he would file a separate suit on behalf of Maglie.

Chandler, responding to the series of hearings that were going on around him and Organized Baseball, said:

> (I am) deeply concerned but not deeply afraid (about the court threat to baseball...).
> Baseball does not want to engage in an illegal enterprise....
> Back in 1912 the Supreme Court ruled in the Baltimore case, that baseball was an exhibition.... It ruled that the game was not involved in interstate commerce. Since then we have assumed that we were operating legally.[10]

On the final day of March, Conger declined to direct Organized Baseball to reinstate Lanier and Martin. The players had requested an injunction that would require them to be allowed to return to work. The judge believed that an injunction was intended to enable a situation to retain the status quo rather than provide an action that would change it. Allowing the pitchers to return would have altered the situation.

On April 5, Herlong and Mills announced that Congressional hearings, aimed at producing a bill that would exempt baseball and other organized sports from prosecution under the Sherman Anti-Trust Laws, were scheduled to begin on April 14, four days before the opening of the 1949 major league season. They promised that top players and officials would be invited to testify at the hearings in support of baseball's reserve clause. The two Congressmen both believed that the game needed the clause to continue functioning effectively.

Chandler met secretly in separate meetings with officials of each of the major leagues to discuss the suits and the proposed Congressional action. After the second meeting with American League officials, the commissioner reported that he would not have any further conferences about the matter.

While awaiting a decision from the courts, Gardella agreed to terms to go back on the playing field with the Drummondville, Quebec, club of the Provincial League. Should the courts rule that he could return to playing in the majors, there was a condition in the Drummondville contract that would allow him to leave the Canadian team and pick up his career in Organized Baseball.

A short time later, Conger denied Gardella's request for an injunction that would require Organized Baseball to allow his return to action. The denial was based on the same position that

Commissioner A.B. "Happy" Chandler offered reinstatement to the "Mexican jumpers" on June 5, 1949 (National Baseball Hall of Fame Library, Cooperstown, N.Y.).

had been stated in the case of Lanier and Martin. Johnson, Gardella's attorney, filed an appeal of the lower court ruling, and the situation continued to roll along the legal highway.

On June 2, Gardella, Lanier, and Martin lost their appeals for a quick reinstatement. The Circuit Court of Appeals in New York refused to order the reinstatement of the three players. The decision affirmed the District Court's earlier ruling that to compel reinstatement of the players through the court would restore them to positions they resigned voluntarily.

Three days later and with the court cases for the immediate reinstatement of the players who had jumped to Mexico behind him, Chandler announced that he was granting amnesty to all of the players who had been placed on the ineligible list for having gone to Mexico, and said that he was welcoming them back to Organized Baseball. He said that an application for reinstatement would serve as an automatic reinstatement.

Although the court cases for reinstatement were behind Chandler, the suits by Lanier, Martin, and Gardella were still on the docket. As long as Organized Baseball and the courts were linked, the commissioner and others in Organized Baseball were fearful.

Speaking about the court cases, which he felt had tied his hands with regard to the question of reinstatement, the commissioner said:

> While this situation was still before the courts and could be interpreted as a threat, however, I could not even consider taking such action voluntarily....
>
> The attempt to force immediate reinstatement through the courts has now failed.[11]

Only 17 of the players who went to Mexico and stayed (Vern Stephens, the twenty-third player to leave Organized Baseball, had returned before the suspensions were enacted) were on "the ineligible list." The other five were not under contract or under the reserve clause to a major league team at the time that they went to Mexico. Those who had not been placed on "the ineligible list" were:

Moe Franklin
Roland Gladu

18 ♦ Two More Suits

Myron Hayworth
Charlie Mead
James "Red" Steiner

The players who were returning were promised a fair test by the commissioner. The clubs who had players returning were given an extension of their 25-man rosters. Each of those returning from the suspension would have a 30-day grace period on the team's roster to prove himself to the manager, coaches, and the brass. A player could not be released unconditionally or assigned to a minor league club until the expiration of the 30-day period. However, as soon as a player entered an official game, he would be counted on the 25-man roster and another player on the team would have to be removed from that spot.

National League president Ford Frick advised players who were under contract to a Mexican League team or to any other club to make sure that they received clearance to leave those teams before returning to a major league club. Frick said that the players involved needed to have a letter of release from the league or from the club president so that there weren't suits filed because they left without the proper process being followed.

A number of the players were playing for other teams at the time that Chandler granted them reinstatement to Organized Baseball. Luis Olmo, who was heading back to the Brooklyn Dodgers, was playing with the Pastora team in the Venezuelan League. Outfielder Roberto Ortiz was playing with Maracaibo, Venezuela, and was planning to leave to join the Washington Senators when his contract ran out.

The Giants' George Hausmann and Nap Reyes, the Philadelphia Phillies' Rene Monteagudo, and the Cardinals' Lou Klein were with Mexican League teams in 1949.

Alex Carrasquel, who was under contract to the Chicago White Sox, was playing north of the border in St. John's, Quebec, Canada, after having jumped a contract with Torreon of the Mexican League two months earlier. Lanier, Gardella, Maglie, and Roy Zimmerman were playing in Drummondville in the independent Quebec Provincial League. Adrian Zabala and Bobby Estalella also were with teams in the league.

Mexican Raiders in the Major Leagues

When Lanier received a contract from the St. Louis Cardinals for the same salary he had signed for in 1946, he sent the contract back unsigned and told club president Fred Saigh that he was staying in Canada where he was making more money than the Cards had offered.

Owen was one of the first players to apply for reinstatement, and Branch Rickey said that he would welcome his erstwhile catcher back. Rickey also reminded Owen that Brooklyn already had Roy Campanella and Bruce Edwards, who were both top-flight receivers.

Gardella's, Lanier's and Martin's suits continued in the courts after Chandler's suspension-policy change. On July 5, Gardella's claim for $300,000 was put on the New York Federal Court calendar for trial in November, 1949.

On August 27, Lanier and Martin dropped their suit against Organized Baseball. Maglie, who was considering filing a suit, also dropped his plans to sue. Martin, who was back with the Cardinals, had hurled his team to a 5–2 win over the Giants the previous day for his second consecutive victory for his club, which was in a pennant fight with the Dodgers.

The reason given by the players for dropping the suit was that they were satisfied with their 1949 contracts and working conditions, and were willing to let bygones be bygones. It appeared as if Saigh had spoken with the players, who were both integral parts of the Cards' pennant drive, and that he was influential in their decisions.

Lanier and Martin wrote a letter that said in part:

> In view of our return to active participation in major league baseball, which was the main purpose of the suit brought in our names, we have decided to and have given a general release of all our claims involved in that suit....[12]

Gardella said that he would continue his suit after Lanier and Martin had dropped theirs. However, on October 7, he announced that he was dropping his long-running suit against Organized Baseball. Johnson, Gardella's lawyer, had advised him that he was probably facing a long and costly court battle. Gardella, who was the only player who previously had rejected Chandler's offer of reinstatement, said that he had obtained his release from the Giants, and he would be returning to play with the Cardinals in 1950.

It was later announced that Gardella had received a $60,000 settlement from Organized Baseball. Gardella was back in the major league game after losing some valuable playing years. Organized Baseball was out of the courts, and the reserve clause appeared to be safe for a while longer.

◆ 19 ◆

After the Return

There were varied responses by the players who had left Organized Baseball to play in Mexico in 1946 after Commissioner Chandler's ruling on June 5, 1949, that granted them immunity and allowed them to return to the teams that held their contracts when they left.

Nine players never played in another major league game. They were:

>Ace Adams
>Harry Feldman
>Moe Franklin
>Roland Gladu
>Myron Hayworth
>Charlie Mead
>Rene Monteagudo
>James Steiner
>Roy Zimmerman

Six players made very short returns to the majors and then retired or spent time toiling in the minor leagues. Right-hander Alex Carrasquel put on the uniform of the Chicago White Sox in 1949, appeared in three games, pitched 3⅔ innings, and had a 14.73 E.R.A. before ending his short career with the White Sox. He resurfaced in the Mexican League in 1952, playing parts of four more seasons in that circuit.

Outfielder Bobby Estalella returned to the Philadelphia Athletics in 1949, but appeared in only eight games with 20 at-bats, adding five more hits to his major league total for a .250 average. He was 38 years old at the time, and he ended his professional career at that point.

George Hausmann also returned to Organized Baseball during the 1949 season and played in 16 games with the New York Giants. The second baseman went to bat 47 times during his short stint with the National League club, getting only six hits for an anemic .128 batting average. His next assignment was in the Giants' minor league system.

Left-handed pitcher Adrian Zabala was with the Giants in 1949, appearing in 26 games with nine starts. He posted a 2–3 record, pitching 41 innings with a 5.27 E.R.A.

Danny Gardella, who had started the defections to Mexico in 1946, did not return to Organized Baseball until 1950. His suit had been dropped, he was back from playing in Canada, and he signed with the St. Louis Cardinals. The outfielder played in just one game and had one unsuccessful pinch-hit opportunity before being sent to the minors by his new club.

First baseman Napoleon Reyes also came back to Organized Baseball in 1950 with the Giants. He, like Gardella, also had a one-game, one-at-bat return to Organized Baseball to finish out his career.

Other players had more success and longevity. Infielder Lou Klein played in 58 games with the 1949 Cardinals, who finished one game behind the Brooklyn Dodgers in the pennant race. He batted .219 in his return to Organized Baseball. He was not in the majors the following season, but he was with the Cleveland Indians for two games in 1951 before moving to the Athletics and playing 49 games for them. Klein posted a combined .226 batting average during his final major league season.

Right-hander Fred Martin returned to the Cardinals in 1949, giving a lift to the pitching staff during their battle with the Dodgers for the pennant. He went 6–0, making five starts and pitching three complete games. He recorded a stingy 2.44 E.R.A. The following season, his last, he was 4–2 in 30 games.

Roberto Ortiz, a right-handed hitting outfielder, played in 40 games with the Washington Senators after Chandler welcomed him and the other players back to Organized Baseball. Ortiz contributed one home run, 11 RBI, and hit .279. He began the 1950 campaign with Washington, where he played in 39 games before finishing his career

19 ♦ After the Return

by appearing in six games with the Athletics. He had a combined .202 batting average during his final major league season.

Outfielder Luis Olmo returned to the Dodgers in time to help them capture the National League pennant in 1949. He hit .305 in 105 at-bats during the 38 games in which he appeared. He was in the outfield in four of the five World Series games against the World Champion New York Yankees, batting .273. Olmo finished his career with the Boston Braves, playing in 69 games in 1950 and 21 games the following season.

Mickey Owen didn't make it back to the Dodgers and Branch Rickey in 1949. He finished his career catching for the Chicago Cubs in 1949, 1950, and 1951, and 32 games with the Boston Red Sox in 1954. His highest batting average during those years was in 1949, when he hit .273 for the Cubs.

Left-handed pitcher Max Lanier had five more seasons in the major leagues after his return to the Cardinals in 1949. He went 5–4 that season, starting 15 games during the stretch run. He went 11–9 during each of the next two seasons with the Cards, posting a 3.13 E.R.A. in 1950 and a 3.26 E.R.A. in 1951. He was with the Giants for the 1952 season and began the following campaign with them before ending his career as a reliever in 10 games with the St. Louis Browns.

Of all the players who left Organized Baseball to go to Mexico and then returned to play again, Sal Maglie had the best career after his sojourn in Mexico. It was, in fact, because of his time in Mexico that he blossomed into one of the major leagues' best pitchers during the 1950s.

Maglie had been reunited in Mexico with Adolfo Luque, who had been the pitching coach with the Giants. Luque was Maglie's manager during his two seasons with Puebla, and while the two were together, Luque helped Maglie perfect his curve ball and learn how to intimidate hitters. He became known as "the Barber" because of his willingness and ability to give opposing batters "close shaves." His pair of 20-win seasons with Puebla prepared for him for his return to the Giants in 1950.

In his first season back with New York, at age 33, Maglie was 18–4 with a 2.71 E.R.A. His victories included four consecutive shutouts, which tied the record that stood at the time. He was a league-leading 23–6 with a 2.93 E.R.A. in 1951 for the National League pennant-winning Giants. He started the playoff game against the Dodgers when the "Shot Heard 'Round the World" was launched, but he didn't figure in the decision. He pitched and lost game four of the World Series to the eventual Champion Yankees.

Maglie posted another fine season in 1952, going 18–8 before slumping to 8–9 the following year. In 1954, he rebounded with a 14–6 campaign for the league champion Giants, who won the World Series by miraculously sweeping the Cleveland Indians. He started game one of the series when Willie Mays' outstanding catch of Vic Wertz's drive helped launch the Giants toward their sweep. He left the game after seven innings with the game tied, 2–2. New York went on to score three runs in the bottom of the 10th inning on Dusty Rhodes' home run to pick up the victory.

He was 9–5 with New York in 1955 before putting on an Indians' uniform and going 0–2 with them The remainder of his career which lasted until 1958, saw him playing with the Dodgers, Yankees and Cardinals. In 1956, after moving from the Indians to the Dodgers, he posted his final quality record, going 13–5 with a 2.87 E.R.A. He was on the mound in the World Series opener against the Yankees and picked up the victory in a route-going performance against Whitey Ford. He also went the distance on October 8, but lost the game, 2–0. The opposing pitcher that afternoon was Don Larsen, who also went the distance and fashioned his historic perfect game.

Maglie had eight years in the majors after coming back from Mexico. He clearly outdistanced any other of the "jumpers" both in terms of service and success.

Arthur Daley, writing in the *New York Times* following the $35,000 verdict against Owen in 1952, remembered the events surrounding the Pasquels and the Mexican League in 1946 with these words:

> The entire business was too ridiculous for belief and it causes snickers now. But it was no laughing matter then....
>
> The mystery today is why the majors were so terrified of the league South of the Border. It was strictly a leaky-roof circuit with only one decent ball park, the one in Mexico City.[1]

19 ♦ After the Return

Sal Maglie returned to organized baseball in 1950 and had an outstanding career in the majors (National Baseball Hall of Fame Library, Cooperstown, N.Y.).

Mexican Raiders in the Major Leagues

Daley went on to note that the Pasquels' dream did lead to some improved conditions for players "North of the Border":

> At any rate, the Mexican League was to prove an immense boon to all ball players. Scared owners granted concessions they never would have granted otherwise and the lot of the athletes in the majors is much happier and more lucrative because of the Pasquels.[2]

Chapter Notes

Chapter 1

1. "Landis Announces Code for Baseball Clubs in Dealing with Players," *New York Times*, 17 January 1940, 26.
2. Harrington E. Crissey, Jr., "Baseball and the Armed Services," *Total Baseball, Sixth Edition* (New York: Total Sports, 1999), 2515.
3. Dom DiMaggio with Bill Gilbert, *Real Grass, Real Heroes* (New York: Kensington Publishing Corp., 1990), 203.
4. Geoffrey Ward and Ken Burns, *Baseball: An Illustrated History* (New York: Alfred A. Knopf, 1994), 276, 278.
5. Skip Wachter, "War Wounds," *Sports Heritage*, January-February 1987, 5.
6. Robert Obojski, "Spahn: A Great Pitcher and Personality," *Sports Collectors Digest*, 2 January 2004, 6.
7. Mel Allen, "The True Story of a Hero," *Old Farmer's Almanac, Southern Edition*, 1996. 187.
8. Dr. Willbur K. Brubaker, Letter to author, 1998.
9. Brubaker.
10. Ward and Burns, 277.
11. Ward and Burns, 283, 284.
12. James P. Dawson, "First Dodger Camp Opens Feb. 1 for 190 Service Men and Rookies," *New York Times*, 15 January 1946, 19.

Chapter 2

1. "Sees It Doomed to Fail," *New York Times*, 18 April 1946, 32.
2. David Q. Voigt, "The History of Major League Baseball," *Total Baseball* (New York: Warner Books, 1989), 11.
3. "Baseball Players' Union," *New York Times*, 7 August 1912, 7.
4. "What the Baseball Fraternity Really Is," *New York Times*, 8 September 1912, Sec. 4, 2.
5. "Commission to Get Busy," *New York Times*, 30 December 1913, 10.
6. "Heydler on Tinker Deal," *New York Times*, 30 December 1913, 10.
7. "Baseball Reserve Clause Is Invalid," *New York Times*, 11 April 1914, 12.
8. *Ibid*.
9. "Major Leagues Hit in Chase Case," *New York Times*, 22 July 1914, 22.
10. Ty Cobb with Al Stump, *My Life in Baseball: The True Record* (New York: Doubleday & Company, Inc., 1961), 108.
11. "Federals File Odd Petitions in Suit," *New York Times*, 16 January 1915, 10.
12. "Deny Fed's Charge of Breaking Laws," *New York Times*, 17 January 1915, Sec. 4, 1.
13. "Says Fed's Suit Is Serious," *New York Times*, 17 January 1915, Sec. 4, 1.
14. "Johnson Scores Federals," *New York Times*, 25 July 1915, Sec.3, 2.
15. John Eckler, Esq., "Baseball — Sport or Commerce?" *The Second Fireside*

Book of Baseball (New York: Simon and Schuster, 1958), 108, 109.

16. Gary D. Hailey, "Baseball and the Law," *Total Baseball* (New York: Warner Books, 1989), 644.

17. "Majority Claimed on 6 Clubs by Guild," *New York Times*, 5 June, 1946, 27.

18. "Moguls, Players Agree on Reforms," *New York Times*, 6 August 1946, 18.

19. Geoffrey Ward and Ken Burns, *Baseball: An Illustrated History* (New York: Alfred A. Knopf, 1994), 353.

Chapter 3

1. Jesse Sanchez, "History of the Mexican Baseball," MLB.com, 9 January 2004.

2. Dr. Jaime Cervantes Perez, "The Hot Tamale Circuit, Part II," www.jaimecervantes.netfirms.com.

3. "The Hot Tamale Circuit, Part II," 5.

4. Arthur Daley, "South of the Border," *New York Times*, 3 April 1946, Sec. 1, 35.

5. Pedro Treto Cisneros, *The Mexican League* (Jefferson, NC: McFarland & Company, Inc., Publishers, 2002), 292.

6. Jonathan Fraser Light, *The Cultural Encyclopedia of Baseball* (Jefferson, NC: McFarland & Company, Inc., Publishers, 1997), 449.

7. Paul A. Frisch, "Walter F. 'Buck' Leonard," *The Scribner Encyclopedia of American Lives: Sports Figures* (New York: Charles Scribner's Sons, 2002), Volume 2: 36, 37.

8. Robert W. Peterson, "James 'Cool Papa' Bell," *The Scribner Encyclopedia of American Lives: Sports Figures* (New York: Charles Scribner's Sons, 2002), Volume 1: 70.

Chapter 4

1. Johnny Pesky, Telephone conversation with author, 1 October 2004.

2. Bobby Doerr, Letter to author, October 2004.

3. Dominic DiMaggio, Telephone Interview, 14 October 2004.

4. "Mexican Embassy Heard," *New York Times*, 7 April 1946, Sports 3.

5. Arthur Daley, "Short Shots in Sundry Directions," *New York Times*, 24 May 1946, 23.

6. "Organized Baseball a Monopoly, Mexicans Charge in Court Action," *New York Times*, 17 May 1946, 16.

7. "Organized Baseball a Monopoly...," 16.

8. "Ruth Off to Mexico as Pasquel Guest," *New York Times*, 16 May 1946, 25.

Chapter 5

1. Frank Graham, Jr., "The Great Mexican War of 1946," *Sports Illustrated*, 19 September 1966, 126.

2. "U.S. Ruling Restores Coast Veteran's Job," *New York Times*, 6 May 1946, 24.

3. Frederick Turner, *When the Boys Came Back: Baseball and 1946* (New York: Holt & Company, 1996), 136.

4. Turner, 137.

5. John Lardner, "Fearless Forecast, Spring Edition," *Newsweek*, 15 April 1946, 82.

6. John Drebinger, "And Now the Players Shall Be Heard," *New York Times*, 21 July 1946, Sports 2.

7. Graham, Jr., "The Great Mexican War...," 126.

8. "Chandler Sympathizes with Quest of Ball Players for Improved Lot," *New York Times*, 3 August 1946, 9.

Chapter 6

1. Frederick Turner, *When the Boys Came Back: Baseball and 1946* (New York: Holt & Company, 1996), 16.
2. Turner, 16.
3. John Drebinger, "Gardella Barred from Giant Drills After Tiff with Brannick in Hotel," *New York Times*, 14 February 1946, 29.
4. "Gardella in Mexico," *New York Times*, 23 February 1946, 18.
5. "Mutiny Scare Ridiculed," *New York Times*, 5 April 1946, 29.
6. Treto Cisneros, Pedro, *The Mexican League* (Jefferson, NC: McFarland & Company, Inc., Publishers, 2002), 290.

Chapter 7

1. "Stephens, Browns' Holdout Star, Signed for 5 Years by Veracruz Club in Mexico," *New York Times*, 31 March 1946, Sports, 3.
2. "Stephens Browns' Holdout Star...," Sports, 3.
3. "Stephens Browns' Holdout Star...," Sports, 1, 3.
4. Robert L. Burnes, "U.S. Players Find the Conditions in Mexico Offset Lure of Mexico," *New York Times*, 14 April 1946, Sports, 2.
5. Camille M. Cianfarra, "Pasquel Promises Fight to Finish Against Stephens of the Browns," *New York Times*, 11 April 1946, 36.

Chapter 8

1. Roscoe McGowen, "Rickey of Dodgers Would Sign Olmo," *New York Times*, 20 February 1946, 30.
2. Arthur Daley, "South of the Border," *New York Times*, 3 April 1946, 35.
3. Treto Cisneros, Pedro, *The Mexican League* (Jefferson, NC: McFarland & Company, Inc., Publishers, 2002), 238.

Chapter 9

1. Mickey Owen, Letter to author, 30 October 1990.
2. Roscoe McGowen, "Dodgers Say Owen Is Not on Market," *New York Times*, 16 February 1946, 8.
3. Roscoe McGowen, "Owen Accepts Post in Mexican League," *New York Times*, 2 April 1946, 30.
4. "Owen Returning to Dodgers' Fold," *New York Times*, 9 April 1946, 30.
5. "Owen to Receive $20,000, Is Claim," *New York Times*, 10 April 1946, 31.
6. Frederick Turner, *When the Boys Came Back: Baseball and 1946* (New York: Holt & Company, 1996), 64, 65.
7. "Rickey Is Surprised," *New York Times*, 13 April 1946, 20.
8. Turner, 133.
9. Frank Graham, Jr., "The Great Mexican War of 1946," *Sports Illustrated*, 19 September 1966, 124.
10. "Chandler Awaits Plea from Owen," *New York Times*, 7 August 1946, 21.
11. Turner, 194.

Chapter 10

1. John Drebinger, "Three Giants Jump to Mexican League," *New York Times*, 1 April 1946, 19.

Chapter 11

1. Frederick Turner, *When the Boys Came Back: Baseball and 1946* (New York: Holt & Company, 1996), 125.
2. "Lanier, Lured by $150,000 Offer, Reported En Route to Mexico City," *New York Times*, 25 May 1946, 19.
3. "Couldn't Match Mexicans' Offer in United States, Lanier Asserts," *New York Times*, 26 May 1946, 26.
4. "Mexicans Seeking More U.S. Players," *New York Times*, 24 September 1946, 35.

Chapter Notes

Chapter 13

1. "Feldman and Adams Quit Giants, Sign to Play in Mexican League," *New York Times*, 27 April 1946, 20.

Chapter 14

1. "Players Who Jumped Contracts Ruled Automatically Suspended," *New York Times*, 17 April 1946, 35.

Chapter 15

1. "Players Who Jumped Contracts Ruled Automatically Suspended," *New York Times*, 17 April 1946, 35.

Chapter 17

1. "Lanier Fights Cut in Mexican Salary," *New York Times*, 16 February 1948, Sec. V,
2. "Raids by Pasquel Reported at End," *New York Times*, 12 March 1947, 33.
3. "All Differences with U.S. Baseball Leagues Ended, Says Mexican League," *New York Times*, 23 January 1948, 29.
4. "Organized Baseball Is Held Ready for Peace with Mexican League," *New York Times*, 22 January 1948, 37.
5. "Pasquel Denies Peace Settlement in Baseball's War with Mexico," *New York Times*, 27 January 1948, 32.
6. "Owen Tells Court of Mexican Firing," *New York Times*, 6 April 1949, 41
7. "Owen Tells Court...," 41.
8. "Jury Awards $51,428 to Owen in Counter Claim to Pasquel Suit," *New York Times*, 7 April 1949, 37.
9. "Makes Plea for Owen," *New York Times*, 12 April 1949, 42.
10. "Appeals Court Reverses $51,428 Judgment for Mickey Owen Against Pasquel," *New York Times*, 30 December 1950, 16.

Chapter 18

1. Thomas Ronan, "U.S. Appeals Court Orders Trial of Gardella Suit Against Baseball," *New York Times*, 10 February, 1949, 39.
2. "Stoneham 'Glad,' Wants Showdown," *New York Times*, 10 February 1949, 39.
3. "Chandler Hits Back at 'Peonage' Charge," *New York Times*, 10 February 1949, 39.
4. Arthur Daley, "From Abner Doubleday to Danny Gardella," *New York Times*, 11 February 1949, 30.
5. Daley, 30.
6. "Congressman Fears Gardella's Action May Kill Baseball," *New York Times*, 11 February 1949, 30
7. "Reserve Clause Finds Support Among Old and New Players," *New York Times*, 15 February 1946, 31.
8. "Reserve Clause Finds Support...," 31.
9. "Baseball Exiles Oppose Gardella," *New York Times*, 11 February 1949, 30.
10. "Suits Concern Chandler," *New York Times*, 23 March 1949, 39.
11. "Ban on Major Leaguers Who Jumped to Mexico Lifted by Chandler," *New York Times*, 6 June 1949, 24.
12. "Lanier and Martin of Cards Drop Suit Against Baseball," *New York Times*, 28 August 1949, Sec: 5, 1.

Chapter 19

1. Arthur Daley, "South of the Border," *New York Times*, 31 January 1952, 32.
2. "South of the Border," 32.

Bibliography

Brubaker, Wilbur K. Correspondence with author, 1998.
Cisneros, Pedro Treto. *The Mexican League*. Jefferson, NC: McFarland, 2002.
Cobb, Ty, with Al Stump. *My Life in Baseball: The True Record*. New York: Doubleday, 1961.
DiMaggio, Dom, with Bill Gilbert. *Real Grass, Real Heroes*. New York: Kensington, 1990.
DiMaggio, Dominic. Telephone conversation with author, 14 October 2004.
Doerr, Bobby. Correspondence with author, October 2004.
Einstein, Charles. *The Second Fireside Book of Baseball*. New York: Simon and Schuster, 1958.
Light, Jonathan Fraser. *The Cultural Encyclopedia of Baseball*. Jefferson, NC: McFarland, 1997.
Owen, Mickey. Correspondence with author, 30 October 1990.
Pesky, Johnny. Telephone conversation with author, 1 October 2004.
The Scribner Encyclopedia of American Lives: Sports Figures, Volumes 1 and 2. New York: Charles Scribner's Sons, 2002.
Thorn, John, Pete Palmer, Michael Gershman, and David Pietrusza. *Total Baseball, Sixth Edition*. New York: Total Sports, 1999.
Turner, Frederick. *When the Boys Came Back: Baseball and 1946*. New York: Holt & Company, 1996.
Ward, Geoffrey, and Ken Burns. *Baseball: An Illustrated History*. New York: Alfred A. Knopf, 1994.

Index

Adams, Ace 23, 70, 83, 149–50, 152–53, 171, 181, 189
Alamis, Leonardo 43
Aleman, Miguel 62, 91–92
American Baseball Guild [A.B.G.] 5–6, 25, 37–39, 41, 78, 84
Anderson, Ferrell 112, 115

Ball, Phil 29, 35
Bankhead, Sam 49
Barrow, Ed 13, 16
Baseball Players' Fraternity 27, 29, 37
Basinski, Eddie 20
Beazley, Johnny 16
Bell, James "Cool Papa" 45, 48–49
Benton, Al 22
Bissell, Herbert 32
Blattner, Buddy 126
Bloodworth, Jim 22
Bodie, Gary 17
Bradley, Alva 13
Bragana, Ramon 89, 92–93, 116–17, 156–58, 170
Brannick, Eddie 23, 87–88, 90
Breadon, Sam 13, 38, 76–78, 110, 136–38
Brissie, Lou 18–19
Brown, Mordecai 29–30
Brubaker, Wilbur 18–19
Burns, Ken 21

Callas, Ernestina 44
Callas, Plutarco Elias 44
Camacho, Manuel Avila 62, 89
Campanella, Roy 48, 53–54, 186

Carmona, Ernesto 42, 74, 118
Carpenter, Robert R.M., Jr. 10
Carrasquel, Alex 70, 83, 90, 117–18, 155–59, 167, 170, 185, 189
Casey, Hugh 17, 109
Chandler, A.B. "Happy" 37, 45, 63, 65–66, 75, 77–79, 84, 100, 102, 105, 107, 111–12, 114, 116, 120–22, 128, 139, 161–62, 171–72, 174, 177–78, 182–86, 190
Chase, Hal 31–32, 34
Christman, Mark 97
Clancy, John W. 181
Clarkson, Buster 92
Cobb, Ty 32–33, 64, 179
Comiskey, Charles A. 34
Conger Edward A. 182–83
Cooper, Walker 137
Coscarart, Pete 73
Cramer, Roger 22
Cullenbine, Roy 22

Daley, Arthur 67, 107, 179, 192, 194
Dandridge, Ray 45, 49, 52–53, 57, 79
Danning, Harry 150
Day, Leon 45, 48, 53
De La Cruz, Tommy 57, 79
de los Monteros, Antonio Espinosa 63
DeWitt, Bill 96, 101
Dickey, Bill 109, 121, 155
Dihigo, Martin 4 12, 15, 48–50
Dillinger, Bob 155, 180
DiMaggio, Dom 16, 22, 59
DiMaggio, Joe 13, 16, 38, 74, 109, 155

Index

Dobson, Joe 22
Doerr, Bobby 22, 59
Dolphin, Antonio 43
Doubleday, Abner 179
Drebinger, John 78
Duany, Claro 119, 147, 173
Durham, Tom A. 75
Durocher, Leo 69, 111–12, 115
Dyer, Eddie 74, 134, 136, 138

Easterly, Ted 34
Ebbets, Charles 30
Edwards, Bruce 112, 115, 186
Egan, Dave 47
Estalella, Roberto 58, 70–71, 83, 90, 98, 119, 155, 161–62, 164, 170, 185, 189
Evers, Hoot 22

Feldman, Harry 23, 71, 83, 141–42, 149–53, 157, 171, 173–74, 181, 189
Felix, Maria 41
Feller, Bob 2, 13, 17, 21, 58, 74, 141
Ferrell, Rick 10
Ferrell, Wes 10
Fisher, Geoffrey 21
Flores, Erasmo 170
Flynn, John L. 181–82
Ford, Whitey 192
Fournier, Jack 99
Foxx, Jimmie 10
Frank, Jerome N. 178–79
Franklin, Moe 81, 83, 92, 165, 167, 170, 184, 189
Frick, Ford 38, 77, 177, 185
Frisch, Frankie 46–47
Fultz, David 27–28
Furillo, Carl 105

Galan, Augie 81, 104, 122
Galbreath, Juhn W. 37
Garbark, Bob 22
Gardella, Al 85
Gardella, Danny 6, 23, 58, 70–71, 79, 83, 85–93, 96, 98, 102, 106, 110, 125, 128, 133, 146, 149, 171, 177–87, 190
Gardella, Kate 89, 91, 93

Gardner, Archibald K. 174
Gardner, J. Alvin 63
Gedeon, Elmer 12, 18
Gehrig, Lou 155
Gibson, Josh 45, 48, 51–52
Gilmore, Jim 28
Gladu, Roland 71, 83, 165–66, 170, 184, 189
Goddard, Henry W. 177–78
Gomez, Chile 57, 92, 142
Gowdy, Hank 15
Gray, Pete 20, 60
Greenberg, Hank 2, 12–13, 21–22, 58
Gregg, Hal 104
Griffith, Clark 14, 25, 63, 155, 161, 163
Grove, Lefty 10, 18
Guerra, Fermin "Mike" 111

Halsey, William F. 91
Harder, Mel 38
Harridge, William 22, 38, 177
Harris, Mickey 26
Harris, Victor B. 173
Hausmann, Clem 22
Hausmann, George 23, 64, 71, 83, 125–27, 129–31, 133, 170, 185, 190
Hayworth, Myron 71, 83, 161–64, 171, 181, 185, 189
Hayworth, Ray 162
Hecht, William 68
Hempstead, Harry 30
Henrich, Tommy 109
Herlong, A.S. 180, 183
Herman, Babe 19, 68
Herman, Billy 38
Hernandez, Chico 57, 116
Herrera, Rodriquez "Tito" 117
Herrmann, August 28–29
Hess, Jerome 68
Heydler, John 29
Hofferth, Stew 112
Holmes, Oliver Wendell 36, 177
Hornsby, Rogers 47
Hughson, Tex 22
Hulbert, William A. 26
Hulen, Rubey M. 75
Hutchinson, Fred 22

202

Index

Irvin, Monte 48, 54

Janis, Robert 59, 89–90, 152
Jaurez, Lucas 43
Johnson, Ban 34–35
Johnson, Earl 22
Johnson, Frederic A. 177–78, 181, 184, 186
Johnson, "Indian Bob" 22
Johnson, Walter 32

Kell, George 22
Keller, Charlie 109
Killefer, Bill 30–31
Kinder, Ellis 102
Klein, Lou 71, 76, 83, 92, 133–36, 138–43, 171, 181, 185, 190
Kramer, Jack 102
Kuhel, Joe 38
Kurowski, Whitey 134

Lake, Eddie 22
Landis, Kenesaw Mountain 9–14, 33–35, 38, 84, 114
Lanier, Max 71, 76, 83, 92, 110, 117, 121, 133–34, 136–43, 168–69, 171, 177, 181–82, 184–86, 191
Lardner, John 77
Larsen, Don 192
Lavagetto, Cookie 68
Lazor, Johnny 22
Leonard, Walter "Buck" 48, 52
Logan, Eddie 149
Luby, Hugh 126
Luque, Adolfo 92–93, 128–31, 147, 191

Mack, Connie 18, 42
MacPhail, Larry 16, 23, 37–38, 66–67, 69, 75, 81
Maestri, Amado 119, 139
Maglie, Sal 23, 64, 71, 83, 125–31, 133, 153, 171, 181–82, 185–86, 191–93
Magro, Rueda 142
Maier, Bob 22
Mancuso, Frank 162
Mancuso, Gus 110
Manley, Effa 54

Manush, Heinie 10
Marion, Marty 38, 121, 181
Marsans, Armando 70
Martin, Fred 71, 76–77, 83, 133–34, 136, 138–39, 143, 171, 177, 181–82, 184, 186, 190
Martinez, Conrado 42
Martinez, Oscar 42
Mathewson, Christy 129
Mayo, Eddie 22
Mayor, Agapito 77
Mays, Willie 192
McCarthy, Joe 15, 70
McDaniels, Bookers 118–19
McMahon, Frank 157
McQuinn, George 121
Mead, Charlie 71, 83, 90, 145–46, 171, 185, 189
Miller, Bing 10
Miller, Julius 75
Mills, Wilbur 180, 183
Mize, Johnny 16, 128
Molina, Julio 43
Monteagudo, Rene 58, 71, 83, 155, 157, 161, 163–64, 171, 185, 189
Montoto, Beaver 43
Montoto, Castor 130
Moore, Terry 138
Muckerman, Richard 96–97, 101
Mueller, Les 22
Mulbry, Walter 172
Mulcahy, Hugh 12
Murphy, Johnny 38
Murphy, Robert Francis 5–6, 25, 37, 39
Musial, Stan 2, 13, 58, 74–75, 117–18, 137–38, 180

Navin, Frank 32
Newhouser, Hal 19–20, 23, 96
Niemic, Al 75
Nuxhall, Joe 20

O'Connor, Leslie M. 38, 156
Olmo, Luis 64, 67, 71, 83, 89–90, 103, 105–7, 171, 181, 185, 191
O'Neill, Emmett 22
O'Neill, Harry 12

Index

Ortiz, Roberto 57, 71, 79, 83, 91, 155–56, 158–59, 164, 171, 185, 190
Ott, Mel 86–88, 125–26, 128–29, 147, 149, 152
Outlaw, Jimmy 22
Overmire, Stubby 22
Owen, Gloria 113, 115
Owen, Mickey 64, 67, 70–71, 74, 79, 81, 83, 90, 103, 107–10, 112–23, 133, 139, 141–42, 157–58, 163, 167, 172–75, 180, 186, 191

Padgett, Don 112
Paige, Satchel 48–52
Pasquel, Alfonso 6, 41, 44, 57, 74, 114, 116, 118, 152
Pasquel, Bernardo 6, 41, 44, 57, 63, 67, 69, 77, 92, 104, 129, 136, 138, 141, 162–63, 167
Pasquel, Gerardo 6, 41, 44, 57, 152
Pasquel, Jorge 6, 41, 43–46, 48–49, 51–52, 54, 57–58, 62–64, 67–68, 70, 75, 77–78, 80–82, 84, 86–89, 91–92, 96–99, 101, 104–6, 111–12, 114–20, 122–23, 129–30, 139–41, 152–53, 156–58, 163, 167–75, 177, 179
Pasquel, Mario 6, 41, 43, 56, 69, 77
Patterson, Robert 16
Perez, Javiercito 42
Pesky, Johnny 22, 59–60, 81, 102, 141
Pintar, John 110
Pollett, Howie 121

Reardon, John "Beans" 46–47
Reese, Pee Wee 17, 68
Reiser, Pete 16, 67, 103–5
Rennie, Claire Rutherford 67
Reyes, Alejandro Aguilar 42–43, 171
Reyes, Napoleon 23, 58, 71, 83, 86, 88, 130, 145–47, 171, 185, 190
Rhodes, Dusty 192
Rickey, Branch 11, 23, 45, 60, 68, 75, 104–6, 110–15, 120, 137, 186, 191
Rickey, Branch, Jr. 106, 111, 120
Rigney, Bill 146
Rizzuti, [Scalzi] Frank 97
Rizzuto, Phil 16–17, 67

Robinson, Jackie 48, 52, 59–60, 104–5
Rojek, Stan 103
Roosevelt, Franklin Delano 1, 13–14, 65
Rosen, Goody 105
Roy, Jeanne-Pierre 164
Ruel, Herold "Muddy" 120
Ruth, Babe 69, 179
Ryba, Mike 22

Saigh, Fred 186
Sandlock, Mike 68, 110, 112
Schaeffer, Willie 88
Schoendienst, Red 134
Sessions, Clarence 31
Sewell, Luke 97
Sewell, Rip 37
Shepard, Bert 20
Simmons, Al 46–47
Sinclair, Harry 29, 32
Slaughter, Enos 138–39
Sloan, John 80
Smith, Theolic 48–49
Spahn, Warren 17
Speaker, Tris 179
Steiner, James 71, 83, 165–66, 174, 185, 189
Stephens, Vernon 6, 63, 71, 78, 81, 83, 95–101, 107, 113–14, 161, 171, 184
Stirnweiss, George "Snuffy" 67
Stoneham, Charles 122
Stoneham, Horace 68–69, 75, 87, 90, 126, 178, 179
Striped, Fernando 43
Sukeforth, Clyde 19
Swift, Bob 22

Taylor, Johnny 117
Tebbets, Birdie 22
Terry, Bill 150
Thurston, Walter 91
Tinker, Joe 29–30
Tobin, Jim 22
Trautman, George M. 177
Treto Cisneros, Pedro 108
Triplett, Hooper 82
Trouppe, Quincy 48–49
Trout, Dizzy 22, 96, 121

Index

Trucks, Virgil 21–22
Truman, Harry S 65
Turner, Frederick 75

Valdez, Jesus 42
Veeck, Bill 52
Vinals, Carlos Gomez 43
Voiselle, Bill 150

Wagner, Hal 22
Wagner, Honus 37
Wakefield, Dick 22
Walker, Dixie 38, 105
Ward, Bob 29
Ward, John Montgomery 29
Webb, Del E. 16
Webb, Skeeter 22

Weeghman, Charles 29, 35
Wells, Willie 45, 48, 51
Wertz, Vic 192
Williams, Ted 2, 13, 17, 22, 38, 58–59, 81–82, 141, 168
Wilson, Jim 22
Wilson, Tom 54
Wolff, Roger 59
Wrigley, Phil 38

Yawkey, Tom 10, 38
York, Rudy 22

Zabala, Adrian 23, 58, 71, 83, 89, 92, 130, 145–48, 171, 185, 190
Zimmerman, Roy 23, 64, 71, 83, 125–31, 133, 171, 185, 189

www.ingramcontent.com/pod-product-compliance
Ingram Content Group UK Ltd.
Pitfield, Milton Keynes, MK11 3LW, UK
UKHW042005140426
5217IPUK00015B/1002